Calgary

A not too solemn look at Calgary's first 100 years

Clive E. Bertram
Christmas 1974.

Presented by The Calgary Herald to mark
the Centennial of the City of Calgary, 1975.

CALGARY

text
by
Bob Shiels

This book is dedicated to all those who made Calgary what it is today, to all those who now call it home, and to all those who will call it home in years to come — with gratitude, affection and hope for the future.

Frank G. Swanson,
Publisher,
The Calgary Herald.

Calgary, Alberta, October, 1974.

THE CALGARY HERALD
Calgary, Alberta

DESIGN: Reg Vickers

PHOTOGRAPHIC RESEARCH: Ken Sakamoto

COVER DESIGN: Dick Marquiss

Printed in Calgary by
Smith Grant Mann Alberta Limited

FIRST PRINTING — OCTOBER, 1974
SECOND PRINTING — DECEMBER, 1974

Contents

Foreword

Any community with pride in its past and desire to express its maturing personality should seize upon and use every important anniversary. Canada's 1967 celebrations marking the 100th birthday of Confederation helped greatly to acquaint Canadians with their own history and to awaken them to the richness of their heritage. The year's program was profitable. It would have been most unfortunate if those new interests and enthusiasms had been allowed to starve and die. The challenge was to feed them and ensure their perpetuation.

The Centennial anniversary of the birth of the North West Mounted Police and then their historic trek into what was to become Alberta, helped to nourish and perpetuate that new interest and now the 100th anniversary of the birth of Calgary — a child of the Mounted Police — promises still more.

No city offers more to arouse the pride of citizens and make them smile. And nothing in the city's Centennial year is likely to be more appropriate than this effort to capture and present an added bit of colorful local history, embracing pioneer struggles, reverses, triumphs, fun, and stories about celebrated personalities like James Walker, the Big Four cattlemen, Senator James Lougheed, Mother Fulham, Paddy Nolan, Bob Edwards and a host of others. And nowhere would the self-assigned task of extending that written story of progress rest better than with The Calgary Herald whose unbroken record of service is older even than the incorporated urban community. The Herald was not the first newspaper in the West but it was one of the first and one of the very few to survive for more than 90 years.

For the first eight years after Inspector E. A. Brisebois and his 50 mounted followers rode into the valley and resolved to build a fort, the settlement was an isolated and a shapeless thing, marked by the roughly-constructed log post and a disorganized collection of tents and shacks. But a turning point came in 1883 when under the driving force of general manager William Van Horne, the Canadian Pacific rails reached the Bow River on August 11. Just 20 days later, two courageous fellows with dreams of journalism hung a sign on their small tent pitched precariously beside the Elbow River and announced that they were starting a newspaper. The riverbank location of the tent in which the first issue of The Calgary Herald, Mining and Ranche Advocate and General Advertiser — to give its full name — made its appearance on August 31, deserved the recognition of an historic marker and plaque.

The Herald changed hands a few times and its original name was shortened. Other newspapers appeared upon the scene. Editorial warfare was bitter and entertaining. The town of Calgary was incorporated and treated itself to a civic election. Town politics was stormy from the outset, with some of the leading figures — including an editor — going to jail. But town and Herald from the outset were properly wedded — for better or for worse — and came through 90 years of trial and tribulation and triumph together.

There was the anxiety of the Northwest Rebellion and return of a more normal way of life; ranching flourished and Calgary citizens chose to believe their town was the real beating heart of the industry; a few gold-rush swindles enlivened the community; an Agricultural Society was formed and a fair was held; the town of Calgary became the city of Calgary; Bob Edwards and his celebrated Eye Opener moved in; the city was honored by being named the host for the Dominion Exhibition; there was a truly hectic real estate boom; Guy Weadick, backed by the Big Four cattlemen, staged the first Calgary Stampede; oil discovery at Turner Valley induced speculation madness; like the rest of Canada and the Empire, Calgary went to war, and did it again; a Calgarian became prime minister of Canada; depression in the '30s induced hardship and gloom; the discovery of oil at Leduc brought a new wave of enterprise and expansion and Calgary growth became phenomenal. Steadily, the revitalized city was taking its place as one of the leaders in urban Canada.

It is an amazing story of nation builders and their achievements and every possible effort should be made to preserve it.

GRANT MacEWAN
Lieutenant-Governor of Alberta
1965-1974

Where it all began — Fort Calgary site where the rivers meet.

The way we are

The Family of Man statues frame the Calgary Tower.

Like a lady who can't make up her mind, the city is neither this nor that. It could be a mirage. Prairie cities are like that. You travel through a lot of gopher country, then there they are, shimmering in the middle of nowhere.

But this one is neither fish nor fowl. Not quite a prairie city, it isn't quite a mountain city either. The lady reaches one way for beauty, other ways for wealth, and enjoys the best of both. Maybe she isn't a lady at all.

Two big, elongated geographic features spill down the western part of the map of North America. The Great Plains plunge from Alberta deep into the southwestern U.S. So do the Rocky Mountains. Calgary perches on the line dividing the two.

The original town occupied a snug enclave where the prairies end and the foothills begin. The modern city spills up into the hills and out onto the prairies. The view is (a) vertical or (b) horizontal, depending on which way you want to look. The contrast could hardly be more sharply defined.

The city is closer to heaven than any other major city in Canada. Lest the envious scoff, statistics prove it. The altitude at the Calgary International airport is 3,540 feet above sea level. You have to go to Denver, Colo., or up to Banff to find a loftier setting.

Such a rarefied atmosphere could produce saints, and it has in fact produced both saints and sinners. Calgary has been home to the good, the bad, and the ugly. Whatever the reason, the town and later the city have attracted an unmatched abundance of characters and rugged individualists.

Every city is unique, but few others, if any, can produce so much evidence to prove it.

The mountains seem to rise on the western outskirts. They're really 45 miles away. Seen from the city, the mountain wall averages 9,000 feet. Four peaks stretch above 10,000 feet. Hidden behind the first range is 11,870-foot Mount Assiniboine, straddling the Great Divide.

To the east, the blue of the mountains and green of the foothills give way to the gold of the flat plains. The bald prairie slopes away gently, the horizon is a long, low curve. The impression, similar to what ocean travellers experience at sea, is that of standing in a big saucer.

Perhaps reflecting the area's dominant political hue, the sky is usually Tory blue. Sunsets are normally multi-colored wonders. Below, it's nearly all dry land. There's no ocean here. Despite periodic efforts to fend them off, pigeons outnumber seagulls.

The Bow River snakes into the city from the west, and the Elbow from the southwest. The Bow is the greater of the two. Neither qualifies as one of the world's great waterways. But the point where they meet was chosen for a fort, and that's where the city was born.

It was a logical choice. If the prairie was an ocean, the voyager heading west would strike land where the hills begin. He'd be inclined to leave the sea behind him and the hills ahead of him. He would settle along the coast. Except that the sea is black dirt, short grass, and gravel, the classic traditions of settlement can in a way be discerned here.

From the time the Mounties first saw it in 1875, there was no doubt about where the settlement should be. The site always has had a kind of Lorelei attraction, causing men to rush into the rocky shoals and never want to escape. The mystique endures, though it no doubt was more evident before bulldozers violated the land's virginity.

Many, through the years, perceived a magic about the place. Trying to define it has been an exercise in futility.

In 1879, a visiting horticulturalist from Ottawa, gazing beyond the town toward the mountains, wrote about "the picture which the beholder could feel but not describe." Cecil Denny, an original member of the North West Mounted Police, decided that "only a poet could do justice to it."

It must have something to do with the altitude, and the plains on one side and the mountains on the other. And perhaps it's better appreciated from up above than down in the streets, where opportunities for gawking are restricted by tall buildings and dense traffic.

It's December, the Chinook arch is nearly perfect, and the plane is a single-engine Cessna. The pilot is Ray Scott, manager of the Calgary Flying Club. The flight path is west toward the mountains, then back over the city. The speed is 75 to 120 miles per hour, slow enough for a leisurely look. The altitude is 5,000 to 8,000 feet.

Up here, the mountains are only a moment

A car is wrapped in a snowy shroud following a January storm.

A fortress-like Planetarium, built at a cost of $1.25 million to mark the 1967 Centennial, stands out against the more austere Mewata Armories and the stadium where the football Stampeders once played.

away. Solid, stolid, permanent and always mysterious, they cast their shadows down toward the city. They have that contemplative, near-religious quality about them. Even for those who rarely get up to see them, their brooding presence somehow manages to make itself felt.

Turn around and head back, and the difference is starkly apparent. Ahead, to the east, lies the vast solitude of the plains, broken here and there by a town, a farm, an irrigation canal, or a microwave tower. To the south lies the world's last best cow country, to the north some of the world's most abundant farm land.

Over the city, the 626-foot Calgary Tower reaches up and tries to impale unwary low-flying craft. It's been called a hollow phallic symbol, but it's the city's most readily identifiable landmark. Bow Valley Square stands out among the skyscrapers. In full operation it will contain 10,000 people — a city equivalent to all of Calgary about 1905.

The flight ends at Springbank airfield on the western outskirts. Most light planes now use the satellite field. Those that remain at Calgary Inter-national Airport run the risk of losing an argument with a jumbo jet.

Nose Hill and Varsity Heights reach 500 feet above the airport. They're the high country, and there's still room up there for year-round horseback riding. The low point, within the city proper, is that point where the Bow River slips quietly past the city limits to the east.

On a winter day, when the westerly winds are blowing, the Chinook arch is sharply etched along a curving line. The Chinook is a justly celebrated phenomenon. It's so unpredictable that the weather office has been known to issue two forecasts for the same day, one for the western half of the city, the other for the eastern half.

At its most capricious, the Chinook can push the temperature at Springbank to 35 above or better while the airport is recording something like 5 above.

A lot of meteorological jargon is used to explain why the Chinook winds blow in here, transforming winter into spring and melting the snow. It's simpler to just call it a lot of hot air. On a sub-zero winter day, without worrying why, people

From Nose Hill, Calgary's downtow▸

...oks *deceptively tranquil.*

are content merely to know it's pouring down the hills and heading this way.

The Chinook is the sort of unique occurrence that inspires tall tales. Probably the best known is the story about the man with a horse and sleigh trying to race the hot wind into the city. The front runners were riding on snow, the rear runners were kicking up clouds of dust.

It doesn't happen quite that fast, but it's still impressive. On Saturday, Dec. 10, 1966, the west wind pushed the temperature, in a few hours, from 8 below to 40 above. Unfortunately, it can end as quickly as it begins. On Dec. 30, 1933, from a high of 40 above, the temperature dropped 30 degrees in about 10 minutes, and the low that night was 5 below.

The climate generally is classified as cold temperate — cold because the city is pretty far north, temperate because of the Chinook and the high elevation.

The record high temperature (in July, 1919, and July, 1933) is 97. The record low (in February, 1893) is 49 below. It can get a lot hotter downtown, but the official reading at the airport never has reached 100.

The average annual wind speed is 10.5 miles per hour (less than Winnipeg, much more than Vancouver). The city basks in an average of six hours of sunshine daily. Rainfall averages a moderate 17.19 inches per year. The average frost-free period is a short 109 days.

But all this varies spectacularly. It's highly unpredictable, and everything isn't always what it appears to be. Unusual atmospheric conditions — and in Calgary the unusual is normal — frequently combine to create a mirage. The illusion is so strong it seems to move mountains.

The story is told about some U.S. soldiers stationed here during the Second World War. Quartered at Currie Barracks, they got up one clear, summer morning, and decided to walk over to the mountains before breakfast. A truck rescued them, still 15 miles from their destination, about 3 in the afternoon.

In this part of the world, great distances are accepted as a fact of life. If westerners are notoriously high-speed highway drivers, it's because they have so far to go before they arrive anywhere.

From Calgary it's 182 miles to Edmonton, 826 miles to Winnipeg, 620 miles to Vancouver, 201 miles to the U.S. border, 473 miles to Spokane, Wash., and 1,163 miles to mile-high Denver, Colo. — but only 77 miles to Banff, which, comparatively, is no distance at all.

Going backward, it's a much shorter trip. In terms of time Calgary is a mere infant. The city celebrates its Centennial in 1975 — only 100 years of history. The country is eight years older than the city.

The town was shaped by Mounties, Indians, cowboys, railroad builders, settlers from all over. The result was a rambling, gambling town, transformed but not completely changed by the oil men who came later. They were gamblers too. The town's most successful citizens have always been those who knew how to take a pratfall, get up, and try again.

Today the tall buildings keep getting taller, and the suburbs keep probing everlastingly outward. The game goes on, for ever bigger stakes. It could be just another big city, but it isn't. If the lady is a tramp, and in some ways she is, she still has class.

The celebrated force of 300 Mounties that headed west from Manitoba in 1874 came gunning for whisky traders. In 1875 a 50-man contingent discovered the confluence of the Bow and Elbow Rivers, and set up a camp there. That was the beginning. What's happened since is an extraordinary yarn.

Beginning on the Bow

The Royal Canadian Mounted Police musical ride at the 1973 Calgary Stampede.

Before the Mounties came, Calgary wasn't even a dot on anybody's map. The Indians didn't need a map to find the confluence of the Bow and Swift (Elbow) Rivers. They often stopped here to relax and palaver. There was lots of game, no parking meters, and no high-rises or smog to obscure the scenery.

The Mounties recently devoted two years, not one, to celebrating their own Centennial. The original force was created in 1873. They marched west in 1874. They didn't get around to discovering and naming Calgary until a year later.

As any tourist with a camera knows, the Mounties have an image. It's not necessarily the image they like, but they have it. Much of the blame rests with Nelson Eddy and a 1936 Hollywood movie called Rose Marie. Resplendent in scarlet and gold, and singing of his love for Rose Marie, Nelson Eddy became Everyman's archetypical Mountie.

It never was quite like that. There's no record that the original Mounties ever stopped in the wilderness to sing. And the prairie dust soon tarnished their scarlet and gold uniforms. If the Mountie still emerges larger than life, it's because a mere 300 of them actually were able to "tame" the Canadian West. In the process they probably saved it for Canada.

A great gaping vacuum existed. For 200 years the Hudson's Bay Company held a charter to trade in the unexplored area of North America. Prince Rupert, a cousin of the king, held shares in the company, and the whole vast region was duly dubbed Rupert's Land. Then, in 1870, the company turned over sovereignty of Rupert's Land to the three-year-old Dominion of Canada.

It was quite an acquisition. Trying to cope, the Dominion carved out a little province called Manitoba along the Red River. Everything to the north and west became the North West Territories. Nominally under Canadian rule, it was still Indian and buffalo country, and nobody except the Indians and the buffalo knew very much about it.

In the 1870s, London, England, was very much the de facto capital of the world. Queen Victoria presided over an empire upon which the sun daren't set. The U.S. wasn't enjoying a good

15

decade. President Ulysses S. Grant, the hero of the civil war, presided over two administrations beset by economic woes and scandals.

Horace Greeley was telling young men to Go West, and a lot of young men were listening to him. They were going not only west but also north. The 49th parallel, a figment of some Englishman's imagination, didn't mean anything to them.

The great buffalo herds were on their way to being wiped out. Tanned buffalo hides helped turn the wheels of industry in the eastern U.S. They were building railroads across the U.S., and the construction crews needed meat. The Indians had the buffalo, the newly-arrived traders had whisky.

Sir John A. Macdonald, alarmed by reports coming in from Hudson's Bay traders and missionaries, decided in 1873 to send 150 men out there to show the flag (the Union Jack) and chase any freebooting foreigners in the vicinity back home.

Sir John originally called his new force the North West Mounted Rifles. But that made the Americans nervous. Sixty years earlier, following the War of 1812, Britain and the U.S. had mutually agreed they wouldn't station any armed force along the border. Tactfully, Sir John changed the name to the North West Mounted Police. It was the same bunch as before, but the Americans were placated.

Before the Mounties went west, they increased the force to 300 men. One man to about 2,000 square miles seemed adequate to those who intended to remain in Ottawa. A rule of thumb at the time was that any one Canadian could whip any four Yanks.

Requirements weren't too stringent. Preferably, recruits should be "of sound constitution, able to ride, active and able-bodied, of good character and between the ages of 18 and 40 years, and able to read and write either the English or French language."

They wound up with a motley collection of soldiers and farmers, clerks, tradesmen and telegraph operators, professors and students, bartenders, lumberjacks, and some who were just fun-seekers with time on their hands. The salary was $1 a day for constables, 75 cents for sub-constables, and there was nowhere to spend it.

The kick-off point for the Great March West was Fort Dufferin, near the U.S. border 60 miles south of Winnipeg. The journey was to last three months and cover 800 miles.

What was happening in Canada was quite different from what happened in the U.S., where the settlers arrived as often as not ahead of the law. The result there was a Wild West characterized by Tombstone, Dodge City, Wyatt Earp and Doc Holliday. The fact that in Canada the law arrived ahead of the settlers made a world of difference. People still got shot, but not so often, and they

NWMP scouts at Fort Macleod in 1890: Cecil Denny is on the far left.

mostly were the kind of people who probably would have got shot wherever they went.

There are all kinds of romanticized pictures of the Mounties in their scarlet tunics, white pith helmets, pillbox caps, long brown boots and white buckskin gauntlets, riding majestically across the plains. They may have looked like that when they started out, but there was no way they looked like that after crossing a few miles of wind-blown prairie.

Before they ever left Fort Dufferin, they almost lost all their horses. A bolt of lightning landed smack in the middle of their herd, in the middle of the night, and they spent the rest of the night and the following day chasing their transportation. The net loss, though, was just one horse.

The journey west finally got started July 8, 1874. The 300-man force was divided into six 50-man troops. They brought with them 310 horses, 142 oxen, 93 cattle, 114 Red River carts, 73 wagons, 2 muzzle-loading field guns and 2 brass mortars. Laboriously hauled all the way from Fort Dufferin to Fort Macleod, the field guns and mortars turned out to be a waste of everybody's time. They were never fired in anger.

For the thin red line it quickly became a question of surviving. The force fought dysentery and typhoid fever. The pillbox caps were ridiculous. Later, as soon as they got a chance, the sun-blistered recruits dug into their pokes to buy plain cowboy hats.

The man in charge was Commissioner George Arthur French, and he had a problem. He was lost. No road maps, no roads, no nothing. The destination was the notorious whisky-trading post, Fort Whoop-Up. It was up ahead somewhere, but where? The expedition began with some Metis guides in attendance, but they soon got lost, too, and simply decided to go back home.

Calculating, correctly, that, whatever else, the U.S. must be somewhere to the south, French and Assistant Commissioner James Farquharson Macleod left the main force behind and set out with a small party of men to find Fort Benton, known to be situated somewhere along the Missouri River.

French and Macleod reached Fort Benton on Sept. 24, 1874, and found there a thriving U.S.-style frontier city. They acquired badly-needed fresh horses and supplies. Equally important, they

Jerry Potts was said to have a map of the frontier in his head. He led the Mounties deep into Alberta in 1875.

acquired someone who could tell them (a) where they were and (b) where they were going.

Jerry Potts, the celebrated half-breed guide who was to serve with the Mounted Police for 22 years, looked like something the goat dragged in: small, pinched features, round shoulders, bow legs, pigeon toes, an untrimmed stubble of whiskers, a lop-sided little character with, it was said, "an undue fondness for firewater."

His vocabulary was limited to "yup" and "nope" and not much else. Posterity records only one immortal quotation. Someone asked him what was on the other side of a hill. "Nudder hill," Potts replied.

But Jerry Potts had a map of the frontier country inside his shaggy head. He got the job done for the North West Mounted. While French headed back north and east on a separate expedition, Potts led Col. Macleod to his destination near present-day Lethbridge. The stage was set for the historic Battle of Fort Whoop-Up.

Macleod unlimbered his field guns and mortars and trained them on the whisky-traders' stockade. He and Potts rode boldly forward, establishing a lasting tradition of bravery above and

beyond common sense. Loudly, they announced their readiness to do battle. They pounded on the door.

A tall, thin, goateed American opened the door and invited them in. His provisions weren't grand, he apologized, but could they stay for dinner anyway? He had some fresh vegetables from a little garden there.

Thus ended the Battle of Fort Whoop-Up. The whisky-traders, lacking any tradition of bravery, were long gone.

Macleod pressed on a few miles west and established his first fort on a low-lying island in the shallow Oldman River. He called it Fort Macleod. The early commanders weren't immodest about committing themselves to posterity. Later, James M. Walsh would lend his name to Fort Walsh, southwest of Maple Creek in the Cypress Hills, and Samuel Benfield Steele would lend his to Fort Steele, beyond the Crow's Nest Pass near the present site of Cranbrook, B.C.

The first winter came and went, and the Mounties finally got around to discovering Calgary in 1875. Again, they took a round-about approach. Even with Potts, they seemed incapable of going anywhere in a straight line.

Before the police were even half-way established in the West, bureaucracy being what it is, the federal government sent Major-General Edward Selby-Smyth, commander of the Canadian militia, out here on an official tour of inspection.

George Clift King was the first white man to set foot on the south bank of the Bow River.

F Troop of the North West Mounted Police lines up outside Fort Calgary in 1876.

In August, 1875, Selby-Smyth was at the Red Deer River looking for something to inspect. Macleod obliged with a force that forded the Bow River 30 or 40 miles upstream from the Bow-Elbow confluence. With Jerry Potts' help, they arrived at the Red Deer River, and an inspection was duly held.

The trip took the Mounties through the heart of the buffalo country. Diaries recorded that there were bison everywhere, and bluffs and woodlands, little lakes and sloughs "that were alive with ducks." And mosquitoes that rose in "torturing clouds." The men lit smudge pots to fend them off.

With Selby-Smyth more or less placated, Macleod was free to turn his attention to establishing a new fort somewhere between Fort Macleod and the Red Deer country. He sent sub-Inspector Ephraim A. Brisebois and a force of 50 men back south to finally set down roots on the site that would become Calgary.

It's rather unfortunate that the division that first set foot on Calgary-to-be was identified as F Troop. Many still remember a particularly ridiculous Hollywood television series of the same name that had a long run during the 1960s. In the tv version, F Troop (of the U.S. Cavalry) spent most of its time falling off the lookout tower and helping the Indians sell a home-brewed brand of primitive rotgut.

Freshly scrutinized by Selby-Smyth, F Troop (of the North West Mounted) probably was a pretty good-looking crew. Each troop at that time prided itself on its own distinctively-colored mounts. Late in August, 1875, F Troop sat astride 50 snorting light bays along the crest of the North Hill.

The exact location was one or two blocks east of Centre St. Bridge. The force, of course, hadn't come looking for Centre St. Bridge. It wasn't built yet. Anyone intending to cross a river could expect to get wet. Even the Bow at low tide was an obstacle.

Lawrence H. Bussard, of the history department, University of Alberta, wrote a thesis on the early history of Calgary in 1935. He described the scene as the Mounties saw it from their vantage point on the North Hill as follows:

"Before them was a spacious valley through which two good sized rivers wound their way: the Bow from the west, the Swift (Elbow) from the southwest. The site of the present city was covered with long grass and the numerous small lakes were literally swarming with wild fowl. The river banks were heavily timbered on the south side; the present Victoria Park was covered with large cottonwood trees, as was a large island in the Swift which was washed away in 1885. A colony of beavers had built a large dam across the Swift and it had flooded much of the land south of the present C.P.R. . . ."

Many of the Mounties there that day wrote down their impressions of what they saw. Cecil

Denny wrote that "the view amazed us. Before us lay a lovely valley, flanked on the south by rolling hills. Thick woods bordered the banks of both streams. To the west towered mountains with their snowy peaks."

Others told of "silvery waters, rolling uplands, and to the east the bare loneliness of the plains where countless bison wandered in undisturbed procession." The prairies were "flower-perfumed," there was plentiful timber and water, and "good land to grow oats, potatoes, pasture and hay."

Only one detail detracted from the idyllic scene. Down on the flats, a buffalo-skin death lodge "bore silent witness to a recent fight between Indians and whisky desperadoes." Up the Elbow, they later would find the charred timbers of a small trading shack wiped out by the Blackfoot.

The Mounties possibly misinterpreted the significance of the death lodge. The Blackfoot never buried anyone under the earth. If a man died in his tepee, the tribe would sew up the flaps, place branches around it to fend off wild animals, and leave it to rot. The man's spirit was believed to still dwell within the tepee. The "death lodge" became his tomb.

The Mounties' immediate concern was to build a fort before winter set in. The site seemed obvious — down low near the junction of the Bow and the Swift (the name was changed later when someone noticed that the Swift, zig-zagging uncertainly, looked somewhat like somebody's elbow).

Brisebois led his men down a steep embankment to the Bow. They forded the river about where the Langevin Bridge is today. Supply wagons were floated across. George Clift King was the first to set foot on the south bank west of the Elbow. In 1886, a grateful citizenry would elect him mayor.

By September, 1875, Calgary was still a tentative entity. Awaiting reinforcements, the men of F Troop may have had second thoughts about their splendid situation. Making do with what they had, they pitched tents, dug trenches, covered them with earth and brush, gathered firewood, and during the cold nights huddled six to eight men together inside these crude shelters.

No one in Eastern Canada had told them when they signed up that their new home on the range would be like this. The fun-seekers among them probably were thinking about applying for a refund.

Sgt. Frederick Augustus Bagley was a bandmaster in the North West Mounted Police. Posted in Calgary, he posed with the troop's "best friend" in this 1884 photo.

A fort to call home

Fort Calgary in 1875: Mountie's sketch appeared in Canadian Illustrated News in 1881.

The fear, real or imagined, that the Americans can come up here and take over just about anything worth owning, particularly natural resources, has preoccupied Canadian nationalists for many years. Sir John A. Macdonald worried about it in the 1870s. That's why he sent the Mounties west — to head off the invaders before they established squatters' rights over everything.

Initially, however, the Mounties themselves weren't in a position to harbor any such qualms. For them, there were more immediate and practical considerations. Having chased the American interlopers home to Montana, they turned right around and welcomed them back.

Huddled in their trenches in the September chill, the Mounties urgently needed a home they could call their own. The experienced builders (of whisky forts and army outposts) were in Fort Benton, Montana. They were up here building Fort Calgary almost as soon as the Mounties arrived. With winter crowding in, there was no time to fuss about their nationality.

Without Fort Benton there couldn't have been a Fort Calgary. Not, in any event, in 1875. Earlier, Fort Benton had been the supply base for the whisky traders. After the Battle of Fort Whoop-Up, where, if nothing else, the Mounties made their presence known, the old freebooters to the south acquired an overnight taste for legitimate trade.

Their leader was Isaac Gilbert Baker, a trader operating out of an imposing two-storey building in beautiful downtown Fort Benton. He noted the advent of the Mounties earlier (back when they got lost while trying to find Whoop-Up) and deduced that both they and the settlers who would follow them would need supplies. A shrewd fellow, he was ready, willing and able to supply anything anybody needed for cash or credit.

Fort Benton isn't much today, but back in the 1800s, the fort was a boistrous, thriving place at the tag-end of a Missouri River trade route stretching all the way to St. Louis and the Mississippi. Sternwheeler ships docked there, and it wasn't unusual to see 1,000 oxen loading on the main street.

The town attracted fortune hunters, desperadoes and gunslingers. But there always was a small core of more-or-less legitimate business men. I. G. Baker had put together an incredibly diverse and far-flung business empire. If the price was right, free-enterprising I. G. Baker Company men would go anywhere and do anything.

As the Mounties branched out, establishing new forts, Baker's crowd tagged along. They built forts under contract and hauled in everything from tea to bullets from the warehouses and levees at Fort Benton. Ironically, the route they used was the old whisky runners' route, the Whoop-Up Trail.

I. G. Baker's ox teams creaked up to the Bow and Elbow junction about two weeks after the Mounties got there. If Brisebois and his men recognized any former whisky traders among the bull-whackers, they didn't say anything. What mattered was that the wagons bore food, winter clothing, and stoves.

Then they built the fort. They cut 14-foot pine logs six miles up the Elbow and floated them downstream. They dug trenches marking out a rectangle. Logs placed upright in three-foot ditches formed the outer pallisade. Facing inward were two large barracks, a quartermaster's store, a guard room, two large stables, and assorted workshops. The fort, set on a low, flat plateau somewhat back from the point where the rivers met, extended 200 feet long by 150 feet wide.

A farmer, John Glenn, who with another farmer, Sam Livingston, and a priest, Father Leon Doucet, were the only white men in the area when the Mounties arrived, provided the finishing touch. Using "good building stone found in the river," he built fireplaces in each of the buildings.

The Mounties and their horses moved in, stomping the cold out of their feet and competing for a place close to a fire. Baker's boys moved out, but not far. A short distance south of the fort, they threw up a low, 100-foot-long company store. The settlement was acquiring a permanent look, like it might be here to stay.

But, if it wasn't one thing it was another. The next settlers were totally unexpected. Mice, attracted by the new store and its goodies, threatened to overrun the place. Then, through some fluke of fortune, a would-be settler from Ontario wandered in — and he brought a cat with him. A Baker man traded a good horse to get that cat. And the cat ate the mice.

With the Great Mouse Scare under control, the Mounties and the Baker bunch had, in a relatively short period, secured the territory west of the Elbow.

With the I. G. Baker Company on the scene, it followed that the ubiquitous Hudson's Bay Company wouldn't be far behind. It wasn't. Alerted to the situation by pioneer missionaries George and John McDougall, a Hudson's Bay factor situated up the Bow at Ghost River, where business was bad due to no customers, packed up his whole store and moved it downstream.

Trading goods from Edmonton and flying the British, not the American flag, the Bay quickly set up shop and added a manager's residence. I. G. Baker would make a good fight of it for many years to come, but in time the Bay, originally located across the river on the east side of the Elbow, would chase him back home to Montana.

By the time the first building boom had run its course, the community consisted of the fort, the Baker and Hudson's Bay stores, a few shacks, a small church built by John McDougall, and some tents occupied by assorted camp followers. In his diary, one of the original Mounties called it "the Garden of Eden."

The matter of what to call it in fact remained to be resolved. The area was known simply as The Elbow. Surveying his domain, Inspector Brisebois decided something more inspiring was needed.

Mulling it over, he came up with an answer that, to him at least, was as plain as the moustaches on everybody's face. To the men of F Troop assembled in their banquet hall he announced that henceforth the place would be known as Fort Brisebois.

If he expected applause, there wasn't any. The idea landed with a dull thud. Petulantly, Brisebois stuck by his guns. And Fort Brisebois it was, for several weeks, until word of the christening got back to Col. Macleod.

Situated as he was in Fort Macleod, a case could be made that James Farquharson Macleod was living in a glass house. Regardless, he wasn't buying Fort Brisebois. A letter, signed by Major A. G. Irvine, was sent to Ottawa, dated Feb. 29, 1876. It said nobody wanted Brisebois as the name for the new fort and implied that no one except Brisebois could pronounce it.

Instead, Col. Macleod recommended Calgary. That's how Irvine spelled it in his original letter. Somewhere along the way, someone added a second "r" and it became Calgarry. This confused the issue briefly. But Calgary was the name eventually decided upon, and Calgary it has remained.

There are several versions of what the name means. Col. Macleod's Scottish cousins had an estate called Calgarry on the Isle of Mull. Irvine said he understood it meant "clear running water." In Gaelic, however, the word seems to break down

Inspector Ephraim A. Brisebois led the men of the North West Mounted Police across the Bow. Later he wanted to name the little settlement Fort Brisebois.

The I. G. Baker store in the early 1880s shows rapid growth from a modest beginning.

into "cala" (a harbor) and "airigh" (arable pasture land). Go back even further and there's a Norse version describing "an enclosure for calves."

Clear running water has remained the most popular translation. Arable pasture land beside a harbor or an enclosure for calves never really caught on.

It was too bad, though, about poor Brisebois. He really was the founder of the city.

One account has him, before coming to Canada, fighting in Italy as a member of the French Zouave, a celebrated 19th-century infantry unit. He first turns up in Canada recruiting men for the North West Mounted in New Brunswick and Nova Scotia. During the march west, he commanded B Troop. He may not have been too popular with his fellow officers. One described him as "inclined to be insubordinate and make difficulties about trifles."

He was only 25 years old when he led F Troop to Calgary in 1875. The decision to call the place Calgary apparently didn't sit well with him. He left the force in the summer of 1876 to become a registrar of land titles.

If he were around today, he might be heartened to know that he isn't entirely forgotten.

Brisebois Drive, in northwest Calgary, bears his name.

Not much happened in Calgary (nee Brisebois) after 1876. As late as 1881, the population still was a mere 75. At one point Ottawa considered selling the land to the neighboring Cochrane Ranch. But the sale didn't go through. Various detachments of Mounties, large and small, came and went, but the fort remained.

An idea of what life was like in the very early days can be culled from diaries and from reports sent back to Ottawa. Selby-Smyth, the militia commander, painted a cheerful picture. There were hardships, but "they (the men) breathe the clear pure air of mountain or prairie, sickness is about unknown, and they know they are pioneers in a rich and fertile territory."

A different view emerges from a diary kept by Simon John Locke, who served with the Mounties in Forts Macleod and Calgary from 1876 to 1882. In Fort Macleod he wrote:

"Jan. 1: A dance in Martin's Hall and a good many were drunk on Jamaica Ginger . . . Christmas Night; a fight took place between the police and the citizens, had a great time in getting things quieted down . . . Police boys

A group of Blood Indians rest in front of Fort Calgary in 1878; behind them, Insp. Cecil Denny, seated on chair and Sam Livingston, leaning on wall.

still playing poker, 10 cents ante . . . I have been sick now nearly three months and on light duty . . . Most of the police were drunk today."

It would be wrong to characterize the force as either saints or drunkards. These were young, adventurous men, drawn from all walks of life. Their Rose Maries were Indian or Metis girls. If booze was available, they might go on a bender. Most of the time it was hard, dangerous work over a vast territory.

I. G. Baker ox teams continued to haul in supplies from Fort Benton. Mostly, they brought such staples as flour, beans, pork, dried apples sugar, coffee, tea, and canned milk. Pioneer horticulturalist John Glenn supplemented the staple

diet with fresh vegetables, a rare summertime luxury, from his considerable "garden."

The rough crowd in and around the fort first viewed the venerable Hudson's Bay Company as merely a quaint throwback to the distant past. One diarist recorded that the company's wares might be suitable for the Indian trade, but not much else.

The Bay, as always, proved adaptable. Soon the company was doing a roaring trade in blankets, boots, caps, underwear, candlesticks, cups and saucers, tea pots, Buckley's magnum toilet soap, leather goods and skins, tins, brooms, lamps and kettles, Lee and Perrin's Worcestershire sauce, Fisher's garden seeds, Perry Davis' painkiller, mustard, "java," and tobacco for chewing and smoking.

There are some sophisticated items in this list. Hints of civilization on the last frontier. And the crowning touch was added, early on, by a reformed whisky trader who set up the ultimate luxury, a billiard hall. He hauled the table in all the way from Fort Benton.

The Mounties still weren't an elegant lot. In 1876, the quality of their dress was being described as "a continuing disgrace." Ottawa, in an inept attempt to cut costs, had arranged to have the police clothing and boots made of poor material by inmates languishing back East in Kingston Penitentiary.

Because the buttons were too far apart, the scarlet tunics pulled themselves out of shape. When the boots got wet, then dried, there was no way to peel them off. The solution: soak them till they were wet again.

The condition of the horses wasn't any better. An official count in 1878 showed there were 201 horses available to all 300 Mounties in the West. Scrawny animals, often too light for the men trying to ride them, they were swapped around from one division to another as the need arose.

In Battleford in 1879, Inspector James Walker complained bitterly that the temperature was 37 below and the water was frozen on top of his stove. But, along with all this, there were moments of light-heartedness. The first Christmas at Fort Calgary in December, 1875, certainly was one of them.

There are numerous accounts of he first Christmas, all cheerful. A Christmas Eve dance was held in the billiard hall. Guests included I. G. Baker and Hudson's Bay Company employees and some Metis tent-dwellers. Music was provided by Mounted Police and Metis fiddlers.

The popular dances of the day were Red River jigs and reels. The ladies were "half-breed lassies in large numbers." Fun and "hearty exercise" were enjoyed by all. Capt. C. E. Denny, an Irishman with a good eye for such details, recorded that the lassies were "not all that bad looking."

On Christmas Day, the non-commissioned officers gave a formal dinner in the mess hall. Armed with "cheap" knives and forks, tin spoons, tin cups and mugs, the men of F Troop sat down around a single huge table and tucked into hearty fare that included buffalo, venison, antelope, canned oyster soup, prairie chicken, plum pudding, mince pie, nuts, candies and coffee.

Not bad, everything considered. They must have been reluctant to break up the party and get on with the business at hand, such as dealing with the Indians.

The Indians were out there somewhere, perhaps gazing down at the festive yuletide scene and wondering moodily who invited these characters to come in and take over one of their better camping grounds. All they knew for sure was that they (the Indians) never invited them.

Calgary in the beginning: rare photograph shows Fort Calgary taking shape at the junction of the Bow and Elbow.

Keeper
of the
peace

Travellers on the Trans-Canada Highway 60 miles east of Calgary mostly don't bother to stop at the historic site at Cluny to read the rustic marker there. It records that on Sept. 22, 1877, the Blackfoot Confederacy signed Treaty No. 7. The treaty caused 50,000 square miles of Indian territory to pass over to the Crown.

Treaty No. 7 was signed at the Blackfoot Crossing on the Bow River, four miles south of the present highway. For the Indians it signified the end of a way of life (nomadic, unhampered) that had lasted for centuries.

The treaty was signed by Lt.-Governor David Laird of the North West Territories and J. F. Macleod, commissioner of the North West Mounted Police, acting as "commissioners" for the Queen of Great Britain and Ireland; by the chiefs of the Blackfoot, Blood, Piegan, Sarcee and Stoney tribes; and by others including Rev. John McDougall, who helped bring the two factions together.

The whites wanted the Indians to open their land for settlement. The Indians agreed to "cede, release, surrender and yield up to the government of Canada for Her Majesty and Her successors forever, all their rights, titles and privileges whatsoever..."

Reserves were assigned to each tribe. The rule of thumb was one square mile for each family of five. A small cash payment was made to each Indian present. The Indians also would receive $2,000 annually to buy ammunition for hunting "as long as necessary."

The Dominion government would provide teachers and cows, hoes, spades, scythes, hay forks, ploughs and harrows, and potatoes, barley, oats and wheat for planting. The intention was clear.

A warrior looks down on Calgary in this painting by artist John Innes.

The nomadic hunters were expected to become farmers. Whether all the Indians who signed the treaty really understood it is debatable.

Today, visitors see the Indians in their finery at the annual Stampede. When the tourists leave, the Indians go home to reserves where they live in houses (not tepees), eat white men's food (not buffalo meat) and watch television. The reserves have hardly turned out to be an unmitigated blessing. They have been called "green ghettos."

Increasingly, the Indians have been seeking their own answers. They no longer hope to turn the clock back 100 years. Neither do they want to lose their identity. By trying to preserve their own culture, many Indians now opt for a set of values perceived as superior to anything the whites ever have had to offer.

The two cultures that came together in the foothills in the 1870s had nothing in common. That they didn't settle their differences with guns is due primarily to the tact of the Mounties and the foresight of one Indian leader. Crowfoot, chief of the Blackfoot, could have wiped out the little settlement called Calgary. He was tempted, but he chose not to do it.

The Mounties' red coats were a deliberate choice. They identified the wearers as the Queen's men and distinguished them from the blue-clad U.S. Cavalry, an outfit that went largely unloved and uncelebrated until the advent of motion pictures.

Any movie-goer imagines he knows about the "taming" of the American West. Wagons drawn into a circle, and Indians riding round and round shooting arrows at them. The stagecoach racing ahead of a mob of pesky redskins. One shot from the Hero, either inside or on top of the coach, and half a dozen of the varmints bit the dust.

Regardless of how much, if any, of that went on in the U.S., nothing similar ever was seen in Western Canada.

The Mounties made the Indians nervous, and the Indians made the Mounties nervous, but there was a reservoir of goodwill on both sides. The

The Blackfoot Treaty is signed in September of 1877. The painting, by A. Bruce Stapleton, hangs in the Calgary Brewery Horseman's Hall of Fame. Chief Crowfoot is speaking.

Mounties could fight if they had to, but they preferred to sit down and talk over the situation. The successes they enjoyed suggest they were amply blessed with the gift of the gab.

Before the Mounties came, the whole region was practically a sea of buffalo. The scene defies recollection. There are stories of horsemen riding for days at a time through a single herd. The buffalo, or American bison, were a big, shaggy breed of wild cattle living off the lush grass that then covered the plains.

The Indians followed the buffalo herds and lived off them. They used the hide for tepees, blankets and clothes, the bones for tools, the dung for fuel, and the meat for food. When the great herds were destroyed, in an incredibly short few years, the Indian was impoverished.

Until then, the Blackfoot Confederacy ruled an empire extending from the Missouri to the Red Deer Rivers and from the Cypress Hills to the Rockies. Once they acquired horses, they were formidable warriors. Their presence here accounts largely for why this finally was in truth the last frontier.

Ronald Atkin, author of *Maintain The Right*, a history of the North West Mounted Police published in 1973, sums up a lot of history in one paragraph:

> "The encroachment of white men and their ways first revolutionized then wrecked Indian society. Horses won in battle made the Plains Indians more mobile, guns obtained in trade increased their hunting capacity and deadliness in war. Another western import, smallpox decimated and demoralized them. Whisky traders reduced them to ultimate degradation and poverty."

Over six decades Crowfoot witnessed and helped shape the transition from the old empire to the new life on the reserves. Tall, lean and dignified, he was everything anyone could imagine a great chief should be. Born in 1830, he acquired a reputation as a warrior. When he died in 1890, he was recognized as the keeper of the peace.

Technically, he wasn't chief of the whole Blackfoot Confederacy, which embraced the Blackfoot, Piegans and Bloods, and assorted allies. He was chief of the Blackfoot tribe only. But it was his influence that stopped the Confederacy from

Crowfoot, chief of the Blackfoot, chose the path of peace and with dignity he led the Indians into a new life on the reserves.

Three Sarcee Indians ride their horses near 7th Avenue and Centre Street in 1909.

confronting the Mounties, settlers, and later the railroad head-on.

Crowfoot could have followed the path taken by Chief Sitting Bull and the Sioux who clobbered General George A. Custer at the Little Big Horn River in 1876. At the time it looked like a great triumph for the Indian cause.

But it was a Pyrrhic victory. Sitting Bull wound up in the Cypress Hills, north of the border in Canada. The Mounties tried to help the refugees in 1877, but Ottawa was determined that the Sioux had to go home. Food and supplies were cut off. Starved out, Sitting Bull retreated back into the U.S.

The low point for the struggling community of Calgary came during the winter of 1878-79.

The population was at its lowest point: eight whites. Chief Bulls Head and a party of 400 Sarcees moved in. They were in a foul mood, demanding food and a new reserve. The fort was unmanned, and the tiny community holed up in the I. G. Baker store. A couple of sacks of flour were offered to the Indians. Bulls Head disdainfully scattered it in the wind.

A force of 13 Mounties led by Inspector Cecil E. Denny arrived in the nick of time. Denny told the Sarcees to move out. No way, growled Bulls Head. So the Mounties pulled down the encircling tepees and hauled them away in a cart supplied by Sam Livingston.

The Indians were too startled to do anything about it. It was a surprisingly typical example of how the early Mounties mixed gall with courage to do what they had to do to accomplish their ends.

Crowfoot realized from the start that he might win a battle but he could never win the war. Hugh Dempsey, director of history for the Glenbow Alberta Institute and author of a biography entitled *Crowfoot*, describes the situation as Crowfoot saw it:

"If the person was helpful to his people, he was a friend. If he was a threat, he was an enemy. It did not matter whether he was white, half-blood or Indian.

"Crowfoot may not have wanted the domination of the white man, but he saw there was no escape from it other than annihilation. He was a man of his era, successfully leading his people from a nomadic life to their reserve without bloodshed.

"Crowfoot, in the fortunate position of knowing the white man's far-reaching strength, chose to greet him as a friend and to extract from him the best possible terms for the inevitable future."

But the road to the reserve was long and hard. Competing with other tribes for what little was left, the Blackfoot followed the buffalo south of the

Alberta Indian leader, Harold Cardinal, meets the Queen and Prince Philip during royal visit to Calgary in 1973.

border. The last great slaughter took place on the Missouri River. Then there was nothing left. Crowfoot led his bedraggled tribe back to the Bow.

It was the white man's home now. Assigned to reserves, the Indians tried to make the most of it. Overnight, these hunters were supposed to become farmers. In the meantime, with the buffalo gone, there was starvation.

The Mounties did everything they could to ease the situation. On one occasion Cecil Denny took it upon himself to buy beef from I. G. Baker in Calgary, pay for it with vouchers, and deliver it to the Indians. Then he submitted an expense account. There's no record that the accountant at Fort Macleod objected.

Though hard-nosed when he had to be, as when he confronted the Sarcees, Denny was about the best friend the Indians had. He could be independently unorthodox, but his chief concern was to see that the terms of the Indian treaties were honored.

A member of the original force out of Fort Dufferin in 1874, Denny left the force in 1882 and served as Indian agent for two years. When a distant relative died, back in Ireland, he became Sir Cecil Denny, sixth baronet of Tralee Castle. But he made his home in the West, lived for a time in Calgary, and died in Edmonton in 1928.

Eventually, the Indians of the North West Territories did become farmers. And cowboys.

Natural horsemen with a bred-in knowledge of the ways of the buffalo, they had no trouble handling a herd of cattle. Many of the first big ranches might not have survived without their Indian cowboys.

By 1884, though altogether new to farming, the Blackfoot on the Bow Reserve had 225 acres under cultivation, including 66 acres of wheat and 27 acres of oats. Without benefit of irrigation, they harvested a crop comprising 5,856 bushels of potatoes, 2,590 bushels of turnips; 426 bushels of onions, carrots and peas.

By 1900, the Indians were adopting white men's customs and habits. An Indian brass band was organized at an industrial school near Calgary. Many were moving from tepees into wooden houses, acquiring bedsteads and washstands. A few took a liking for tall hats and black coats.

If this can be called progress, it continued for a while. At the turn of the century, some sources rated Indian mixed farms on a par with the best farms operated by whites. Locked into the reserves, however, they couldn't grow on a par with the vast irrigation-based railway settlements that followed.

The Calgary Tower today overlooks land once dotted with hunting lodges. All that is long gone. The accommodation reached in 1877 was a marriage of convenience. A century later, after a lot of muddling through, the search continues for the best way to make it work.

Next page: Early Herald cartoonist John Innes found humor in both the Indians and cowboys of frontier Calgary — as well as some of the city's finest citizens.

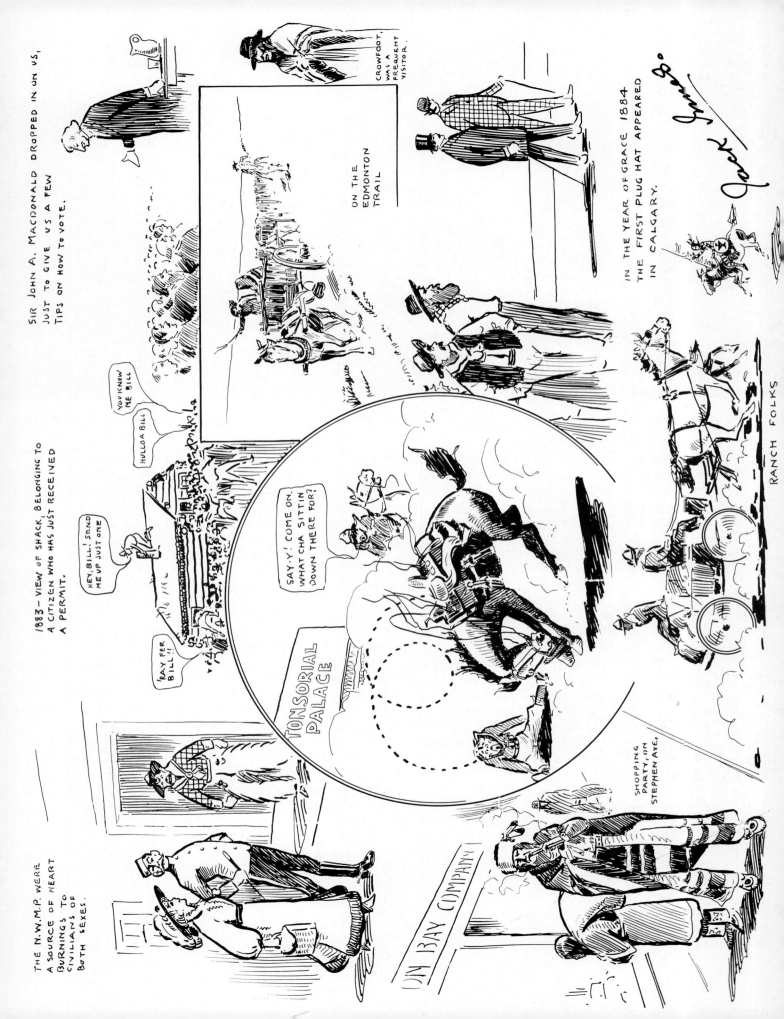

Rough, good men

A ny tenderfoot who wants to call this town a cowtown isn't apt to get much of an argument about it. Fact is, a town like High River has a more legitimate claim to such a designation today. But Calgary isn't inclined to fight the cowtown image. Probably more than anything else, including oil, it's what gives the place its distinctive flavor.

And it's big business. Aside from the packing plants and such, it's the sort of thing that pulls in the tourists. They're bemused by the spectacle of grown men and women playing cowboys and Indians every July.

W. O. Mitchell, author of *Jake and The Kid* and *The Vanishing Point,* travels a lot but always comes home to the foothills country. Make-believe cowboys don't impress him, but he does believe that Calgary's ranching history, despite everything that came later, left its mark.

"The effect of the initial cowmen has a great deal to do with the flavor of Calgary," he affirms. "It accounts for why Calgary is Calgary and not Edmonton or Red Deer or Regina or Saskatoon. Give it another 10 or 20 years, and it probably will be gone. But there remains that quality I think goes right back to those first guys herding their cattle in."

There was a time when the open range extended from Mexico to Canada. But that was a long time ago. As early as 1913, Leroy V. Kelly, a pioneer historian and reporter-essayist for The Calgary Herald, was lamenting its passing in a book called *The Range Men.* "The range is gone," he wrote, "cut up by the fences of the farmers, and the railroad."

Eloquently, he described how it was in the beginning:

Cowboy Clem Gardner on his ranch in 1906.

A cattle round-up near Calgary in the early 1900s: it was a growing business requiring tough men.

"Millions of acres of luxuriant grasses, hundreds of sparkling rivers, thousands of pure springs, rolling hills and bluffs, deep valleys and snug, grassy, well-protected river bottoms — that was Alberta when the Indians owned it and the buffalo chose it as their breeding grounds."

The grass, the streams, and the tree-sheltered valleys indeed were the elements that attracted the cattle men to Southern Alberta. The Chinook was a bonus. Where the Chinook winds blow rarely or not at all, the grass stays frozen all winter under the ice and snow. The Chinook's reach, however variable and unpredictable, effectively defines the outer limits of the cow country.

To the ranchers who first came here, southern Alberta was "the last and best range country." If the buffalo could roam here, so could cattle. The early cattle men were in for some rude shocks, this far north, but they were ornery enough to persist and make it work.

The pioneer stock men were a mixed lot: English gentry, self-made cattle barons, dust-caked cowpunchers, remittance men and tinhorn crooks. The whisky traders who preceded them headed for the hills when they heard the Mounties were coming. The cattle men were a different breed. They came to stay.

Many of the early ranches were English "ranch homes." Better-bred Englishmen, true to tradition, dressed for dinner, organized hunts (for coyotes) and played polo. New Year's balls were held annually in some of the little cattle towns. A cowboy would ride into town with a dinner jacket in his saddle bag. He'd change into formal attire in a stable.

Leroy Kelly found many of these cowboys to be "rough, uncultured and crude." But ranching was a big business "and it required big men to handle it most successfully." Kelly was ready to forgive their little shortcomings:

"The early rancher might brand a stray calf, but his word was usually unquestioned and his statements were his pledges. A man's word was his bond!"

At the bottom of the social ladder, bad men in black hats drifted in here, too — but they were clods. Card cheats, liars, pimps, and the like, they hung around the hotels and bars. If anyone had invited them to slap leather on Main Street at high noon, they would have been out of town before breakfast.

As for the genuine cowboys, Kelly related that they "might go on hilarious 'busts' when in town; they might shoot up a bar-room and smash every light in the place; they might ride into stores on the backs of frantic horses — but they were good men."

Kelly leaves the impression he let his imagination run away with him sometimes. His description of the "good" men leaves his readers wondering what the bad ones were like. As for riding a horse into a store, the doors were universally too low. The only thing such a rider could expect to gain would be a cracked skull.

Kelly could, however, see how the times were changing. Having witnessed the first Calgary Stampede, he complained that the cowboy of 1912 "is not of the same class" as those he remembered from earlier times. There were too many dudes on prancing horses, big spurs clanking, chaps flapping, wide hat jauntily on head — not the real thing at all.

The open range gave up the ghost long before Kelly's time. Covered wagons were creaking up the Oregon Trail into the U.S. northwest in the 1840s, and the decade ended with the California gold rush. Thirty years later, cattle men were looking north because most of the good range land south of the border was long since claimed.

Two disillusioned prospectors, George Emerson and Tom Lynch, herded cattle all the way to Edmonton in 1878. In 1879, they brought 1,000 head of mixed Longhorns and Shorthorns into the High River country. Fred Stimson, originally from Quebec, established the big North-West Cattle Company (later the Bar U) in 1881, and by 1882 High River's cowtown traditions were well established.

Ranchers shipped cattle in from as far away as Mexico. Cowboys arrived from everywhere. Dan Riley, a cowboy who called Prince Edward Island home, came to the High River country in 1883. He was elected the town's first mayor in 1906, and he was appointed to the Canadian Senate in 1925.

Bill Mitchell has an interesting view of the cow man as ecologist. His job was to convert grass into beef. There were no crops, no overgrazing. The cow man "tried to understand what the cow needed. He respected the sovereignty of the cow. He could think like a cow. And he had a higher, wider, handsomer style."

Preparing for an outing in the 1880s: a ranch house at Cochrane.

Cowboys at home on the open range

The 1912 Stampede attracted more splendidly dressed cowboys than usually seen on downtown streets. Old-time cowboys regarded them with suspicion.

These smiling cowpokes worked for the Bar U ranch at High River.

A round-up crew takes a breather: it was 1895 and the cattle drives were part of a big business.

Pioneer rancher Alfred E. Cross set down graphic recollections of what life was like on the range. He wrote about two ranch outfits situated in 1887 at what was known as High River Crossing. They had a good-sized stable, a "stopping house" and a stockade corral. Everything was built of logs.

It wasn't all work: "Poker and an occasional bottle of red eye were the principal attractions. The stage and mail coach called once or twice a week, but the men were not much interested, far removed from the outside world and living so close to nature."

When the poker games broke up, there were long, lonely trail rides. Exposed to all kinds of weather, the prototypical range riders were "lusty, loyal individuals who gave their calling an exuberance and devotion rarely matched."

To A. E. Cross there was "a wonderful fascination about it. If you ever experienced it you can never get free from a longing desire to experience it again."

The first cattle roundup south of Calgary apparently took place in August, 1879. Participating were 16 "indifferent" men and one wagon. Why the men were called indifferent wasn't explained. Regardless, they accomplished something. They demonstrated that, in Chinook country, cattle could survive in the same environment as had the vanishing herds of buffalo.

The cattle men's customers were the North West Mounted Police, the Indians (under their treaty rights) and a motley assortment of early settlers. Not until the railroad came, opening up world markets, did the cattle business become really big business.

But it was big enough and promising enough in the beginning to attract, among others, numerous Mounties. When they left the force they were handsomely situated to stake a claim on virgin land. They had been living off the land for a long time for low wages. Ranching gave them a chance to make it on their own.

The most prominent of them by far was Col. James Walker. In 1881, Senator M. H. Cochrane of Montreal set out to organize a big spread. He incorporated the Cochrane Ranch Company, staked a claim on 100,000 acres of grazing land, and hired Walker as his manager.

The company at this time nearly bought Calgary. The Mounties were ready to write off the place. Had the deal gone through there would be no history of Calgary to relate, or in any case a very different history. As it happened Walker chose a location farther west and the town there, not the town here, bears Cochrane's name today.

For a successful ranch, you need cows. Col. Walker bought an unprecedented 3,000 of them at $16 a head in Montana. I. G. Baker cowboys (who else?) herded them up the Whoop-Up Trail.

A rancher of today moves his herd to fresh pasture at Symon's Valley, on the city's northern outskirts.

The John Ware ranch at Millarville around 1896. At right, John Ware, his wife and their children, Robert and Nettie.

Calgary's early settlers watched in awe as the big herd forded the Bow River near the present Mewata Park, and they listened in shock as Walker raised hell. Pushed too hard, the herd was depleted and worn down. Walker's opinion of the Baker cowboys, expressed at top volume, shivered the timbers on both sides of the Bow Valley.

They tried again the following year. By the end of 1882, it was estimated that there were 12,000 cattle on the range between here and Morley. Many of them didn't survive. The Chinook wasn't co-operating, and the first two winters were exceptionally hard.

But the Cochrane Ranch survived and started taking on the appearance of an empire. Walker, "with military precision," ordered his men to brand everything on the range that wasn't already branded. The Cochrane Ranch had the men, and presumably the guns, to back up its claims.

It looked, for once, like a real Wild West situation. But the other, smaller ranchers headed Big Daddy off at the pass. If Walker was going to round up every stray in sight, they could do the same. They "skipped out" with all the Cochrane cattle they could safely nab. There are no records of any gun-fights.

Shortly thereafter, Walker abandoned the range and moved into town. He built a sawmill in East Calgary, acquired timber rights, and supplied most of the lumber for the first CPR bridges. He became a leading citizen, helping to organize the first school board and presiding over a meeting of citizens that resulted in the community being incorporated as a town.

Alberta Government Telephones' modernistic, elevated mini-park off 7th Ave. bears his name. It recognizes the fact that, among other things, Col. Walker owned and operated Calgary's first telephone switchboard.

Others carried on the ranching tradition, and cattle men still were the leading citizens in these parts. A census in 1884 showed 41 companies and individuals, holding 1,783,000 acres, were in business that year with cattle, horses and sheep. The ranches were huge government leases rented at a modest one cent per acre.

Iowa-born George Lane acquired the Bar U at High River and introduced what were called the finest Percheron stock in America. William Roper Hull brought 1,200 horses through the Crow's Nest Pass and sold them here. He went on to become a beef baron, later selling out to the biggest cattle king of them all, Pat Burns.

In the wake of the first cattle drives, a big flock of about 8,000 sheep from Montana crossed the Bow River in 1884. The traditional conflict between cattle men and sheep men never occurred, mainly because the cattle and sheep men tended to be the same individuals.

The cowboys continued to work hard and play hard. And smell bad. On the trail they couldn't wash or shave, and often slept in their clothes for weeks at a time. They didn't complain about the sheep. They fought the cold in the winter, and prairie fires in the summer, and drew their pay at the end of the month.

One of the greatest cowboys of them all was black. Born a slave, John Ware left South Carolina after the Civil War to become a range rider. They told him to ride at the back of the herd. That's where he was when they brought a Montana herd in to the Bar U ranch in 1882.

A six-foot-three giant of a man, he worked for the Bar U until he could buy his own spread. He became a good family man, good neighbor, and a great cowboy rider. He's been called the greatest rider of all time. No horse was too mean and he was wrestling steers before the idea ever occurred to anyone else.

Big John Ware was killed in a fall while cutting a steer from his herd in 1905. Though he never actually lived in Calgary, he was buried here, and his funeral was the biggest the town had seen until that time.

"He was a white man," Leroy Kelly wrote. In 1905, that was meant to be a compliment.

The good years for the first ranchers ended abruptly with the winter of 1906-07. There had been other bad winters, but nothing like this. Ranchers had come to depend on the Chinook. In 1906-07 the Chinook never came.

They called it the year of the blue snow. Temperatures plunged below zero and stayed there. There was no break. The frost was six feet deep in the ground, and the cattle starved

One estimate placed the loss of cattle in the Calgary district at 60 per cent. Many ranchers went out of business. Those who survived changed their ways forever. Where the homesteaders hadn't built fences, the ranchers did it themselves.

They reined in their spreads and laid in feed. The big ranches gave way to smaller ranches and mixed farms. And the curtain came down forever on a legendary epoch.

Leroy Kelly was nothing if not adaptable. In 1913 he was rhapsodizing about "this grand country, the rich mixed-farming province of the Dominion, the wheat empire, the land of the future."

The railway decides

One of the first trains arrives from Winnipeg.

Sweaty, dusty men laying track across the open prairie near Brooks, 115 miles southeast of Calgary.

1883? No, 1973. They were filming The National Dream, a CBC television series about the building of the Canadian Pacific Railway. At great expense, they achieved a lot of real-looking, old-time authenticity.

Rediscovering the open prairie 90 years after the original railroaders wasn't easy. Southeastern Alberta today, even counting the gophers, isn't densely populated. But, in 1883, there were no highways, no houses, no power lines, no microwave towers, no nothing. The area south of Brooks turned out to be one of the few places left with a wide-open horizon.

The filming of the television show provided a unique chance to see and feel again something of the atmosphere of the railway-building era. In this one remote corner, at least, nothing had really changed. What was it like? A reporter who was there (in 1973) described it:

"Wind howled across the flat land, churning up the prairie soil and turning sunny days into brown-outs. Handfuls of dirt drifted into miniature dunes, clogging equipment. The wind stung faces and whipped words away, making conversation impossible.

"The end of steel in the middle of the boundless prairie inspired a strangely unsettled feeling — a feeling of standing on the edge of the world, of having to work very hard to get ahead, a feeling that technology has its limits, that man very actively shapes his own future."

The railway builders of 1883 must have felt much the same. They were standing on the edge of their world. They were working very hard. They had their doubts about it all. But that greatest of all railway builders, William Cornelius Van Horne, was cracking the whip. He knew man very actively shapes his own future.

Without the railway, there might not have been

A Red River cart drawn by a donkey in Northern Alberta.

much of a future for Calgary. Until 1883, the little community wasn't much more than a way station along the trade route linking Edmonton with Fort Macleod and Fort Benton. The old Whoop-Up Trail was alive and thriving.

Trade was north-south, not east-west. Great cart-trains, or bull-trains, plodded up and down the trail south of Calgary. It's the Macleod Trail now, traced more or less exactly by No. 2 Highway.

In the old days red-necked bull whackers, celebrated for their eloquent profanity, were kings of the road. A three-wagon bull team could carry 15 tons of freight. Slow but steady, they hauled the freight south of here for 15 years.

Along the northern route into the North West Territories, from Winnipeg to Edmonton and south to Calgary, the Red River cart predominated. They were practical — they could carry up to half a ton on box-like platforms and they were built to stand upright, most of the time, on two high hind wheels — but the noise pollution they brought to an otherwise peaceful land was scandalous.

The Red River cart was made entirely of wood,

durable and easy to repair. Because it would have hardened and locked the wheels, the carts employed no grease. Hubs scraped against rough-hewn axles. The sound has been described as "ear-stabbing." The screeching, back and forth across the wilderness, never ceased.

The stage coach was about as sophisticated as anything the early settlers had by way of transportation.

The Royal Mail line left Calgary at 9 a.m. Thursdays, arriving in Fort Macleod at 4 p.m. Saturdays. On Monday it would turn around and come back. There was a regular schedule, too, between Edmonton and Calgary. Schedules were maintained unless the stage got stuck in the mud or the passengers had to get out and help fight a prairie fire.

A typical stage had four horses pulling the coach, six passengers riding inside and four on top. Everybody, inside or otherwise, paid the same fare. Fording rivers, bouncing around, coping with every which kind of weather, no one had time to worry about class distinctions. The passengers

Opposite page: Father Albert Lacombe with Indian leaders Chief Crowfoot, left, and Three Bulls. Lacombe calmed the restless Blackfoot when the railway arrived

The Calgary skyline in 1885: permanent buildings replaced the shacks.

were more concerned about whether they ever would walk again if and when they reached their destination.

To people accustomed to such transport, the Iron Horse was a technological breakthrough of monumental proportions. Calgary awaited the railroad with mounting excitement. Riders drifted in ahead of the rails to stake a claim. Everybody wanted to beat the CPR in the real estate game. They didn't know the CPR very well.

Then as now, the federal government was inept in dealing with the realities of the West. Ottawa had neglected to tell the natives about the big, black monsters pressing against the edges of their reserves. The Indians pitched tents near the right of way and watched warily. Surveyors' stakes laid out during the day vanished overnight. Everybody was getting nervous again.

Again, however, there was no serious confrontation. One railway worker wrote about a large group of Indians riding right into the construction camp. The workers "gave them tea and biscuits" and after a while they went away. No monument was erected to recall that encounter.

Tea and biscuits instead of tomahawks and bullets was possible largely due to the efforts of Father Albert Lacombe, the legendary Catholic missionary who did so much to keep the frontier so surprisingly calm.

An Oblate priest, he had been in the West since 1852, assigned to "coursing the prairies to try and reach the poor savage Crees and Blackfeet." He succeeded spectacularly, mainly because he scrapped the line about "poor savages" and dealt with the Indians as equals.

The earliest missionaries in these parts were rough and rugged frontiersmen, well prepared to cope with any contingency. It's said of Lacombe that once, starving and without food, he boiled his moccasins and buffalo robes and made a stew. It was either the moccasins and buffalo robes or his horse, and he needed his horse.

The McDougall family, Methodist missionaries who worked south from Edmonton to Morley and later to Calgary, were cut from the same cloth. George McDougall died in a mid-winter blizzard. His son David was among the first to run large herds of cattle up the Bow. When the Mounties reached Calgary, his son John McDougall built a little church and conducted services every second Sunday.

Describing him variously as "priest, ambassador, diplomat, voyageur, colonizer and educationist," the Mounties proposed in reports to Ottawa that Albert Lacombe rated a place in history "among Canada's greatest figures." By the time they got through to the sheltering shadows of the Rockies with their scalps intact, the railway builders had good reason to second the motion.

When the first grading crews pitched camp just outside the Blackfoot reserve, and the natives were restless, Father Lacombe was on the scene distributing tea, sugar, flour and tobacco. More important, he was able to explain, as Ottawa never did, what was happening. A bit grumpily, the Blackfoot let the CPR go through.

Now the invaders made tracks fast. Contractors Langdon and Shepard claimed a record, putting down six miles plus 200 yards of track in one day. They started the day with 20 miles of track ready to go, suggesting perhaps that they didn't accomplish as much as they hoped. Regardless,

The first CPR station, in 1884, showed where Calgary would be located.

Langdon and Shepard lent their names to the last two sidings coming into Calgary, and both names have survived.

The village of Calgary then included the Mounties' fort, the Hudson's Bay and I. G. Baker stores, tiny Roman Catholic and Methodist churches, some tents, and two alleged hotels described by one guest as being "not very plausible."

The fort and the Baker store were west of the Elbow River, but the main community was east of the river. The area east of the river was to be the city centre. Land speculation was well under way.

Earthworks, grading, track-laying, ballasting, bridging — the railroad rolled formidably into town from the east. To the east, the Bow River dips straight south. The railroad would have to cross the Bow first, then the Elbow.

With the railroad, or ahead of it, came many of the town's first notables. James Lougheed, after a brief stop in Medicine Hat, moved to Calgary and

opened a law office. William Murdoch, harness maker, hung out his shingle. Later he would be elected the town's first mayor.

Now the railway builders threw a wooden trestle bridge across the Bow River and entered Calgary.

"Hooray!" cried the populace.

Without pausing the railway builders threw a bridge across the Elbow River and kept going.

"Oy!" cried the populace.

Everybody watched and wondered. When the railroad gangs dropped off a boxcar alongside the track, near the present corner of 9th Ave. and 4th St. S.E., and called it a station, everybody became downright alarmed. It was the first indication that the site they had picked for their future city wasn't the site the CPR had chosen.

It happened in Brandon and Regina, and it happened here. The CPR, and no one else, decided where the new townsites would be located. In Calgary, the area east of the Elbow figured to be

Passenger train arrives in 1889; Scotchman's Hill in background.

the site because the area to the west was designated as grazing land for the Mounties' horses.

What no one here knew was that, through some devious manoeuvring back east, the railroad had managed to do the Mounties (and their horses) out of their grazing land. The land west of the Elbow became CPR land. However arbitrarily, it also became Calgary.

The first citizens of the community, unexpectedly finding themselves on the wrong side of the river, tried to put up a fight. The Denny Estate, site of former Mountie Cecil Denny's home south of the Bow and east of the Elbow, was advertised far and wide as prime residential land. But the fight didn't last long.

In January, 1884, James Bannerman moved his flour and feed store across the Elbow to the west side. That decision was fatal. Bannerman also was the postmaster, and he took the post office with him.

The butcher shop followed, then the local jeweller, the billiard parlor, and the alleged hotels. It was winter. They simply put every structure that could be moved without falling apart on makeshift skis and ran them across the ice.

Downtown Calgary wound up situated almost exactly where it is now. The pattern was set. By mid-1884, the new Calgary was an up-and-coming place. More permanent buildings were replacing tents and shacks. Between 1881 and 1884, the population soared from 75 to 1,000.

There wasn't much industry, but there was prosperity. Buffalo bones were selling for $7 a ton as fertilizer in Minneapolis. They had succeeded in annihilating the buffalo right down to the bones.

*Above: Stephen Avenue, now 8th Ave.,
in 1883, or '84. Now there were a thousand
people calling Calgary home. The avenue
was named after CPR President George
Stephen.*

*Below: the tent town that sprang up on
the east side of the Elbow River in 1883.
They watched the railway arrive, and
keep on going west, across the Elbow.
Fortunately, the tents were easy to
pack up and move.*

The railway builders who came here were professionals. Many were Americans who had helped build other lines in the U.S., and many were members of railway operating unions. The labor union movement still had a long way to go in 1883-84, but the railway gave it a foothold.

Though, from the start, the railroad managed to infuriate almost everybody, particularly anybody who had invested in the Denny Estate, there were compensations.

In 1880, eggs were selling for 25 cents each. Groceries of all kinds were in short supply. Crafty storekeepers would try to corner the market in the fall. By spring they could sell sugar and bacon at 50 cents a pound, flour at 25 cents a sack. The railroad ended this price-gouging by opening up a reliable new supply route from the east.

A CPR engineer recalled arriving here in 1885:

"I remember that the evening of our arrival in Calgary some teams came in from Fort Benton and among other supplies they brought half a dozen boxes of apples, the first ones that ever were seen in that part of the North West. It marked an epoch, and as a token of extreme hospitality I was presented with two of them, which I appreciated, as they were quickly disposed of at 50 cents each."

There's a popular story about the CPR board of directors holding a meeting in a private car in Calgary and inviting Father Lacombe to dinner. Grateful to Lacombe for all he had done, they made him president of the railway for an hour. Lacombe then named CPR president George Stephen head of the Calgary parish of St. Mary, and voted himself two life-long passes to travel on the trains.

There seems to be no record in the CPR archives that any such meeting ever took place. So the story may or may not be true. In any case, if one story about Father Lacombe doesn't hold up there's always another.

He did, somewhere along the way, acquire a CPR pass. Having long since moved up the Elbow and built a new church in the Mission district, he wanted to formally claim the land. Using his pass, he went to Ottawa.

In Ottawa the missionary in his tattered cassock encountered a bureaucrat who told him he could have the land, but he would have to wait a couple of weeks for the red tape to be processed. Lacombe said fine, he would wait right there on the carpet. He had camped out under a lot worse circumstances.

The bureaucrat forwent the red tape. Lacombe got his land. And the CPR forwent the usual freight charge for shipping out a new bell for his church.

The box car served only a short time as the CPR depot. A two-storey shack replaced it near the site of the present Palliser Hotel. A muddy plank connected the station with the platform. Then they built the fine sandstone depot and dining room at Centre St., and that lasted until Palliser Square transformed everything.

The first passenger service started in December, 1883, between Calgary and Winnipeg. Trains didn't stop long here because Canmore, not Calgary, was the divisional point. The first transcontinental train puffed through in 1886. Among the passengers were Sir John A. and Lady Macdonald.

West of Calgary, Lady Macdonald made history of sorts by riding the prime ministerial train in a chair attached to the cowcatcher in front of the locomotive. Sir John remained in his private car and ordered another double Scotch and soda. Despite the precedent, riding the cowcatcher never caught on.

And west they came

The Colonist car played a vital role in the movement west.

The federal system of government in this country is like most marriages. The partners fight a lot. When an emissary from Ottawa appears on the western horizon, the natives draw their wagons into a circle and make threatening gestures. Experience has taught them to beware of carpetbaggers.

This attitude of extreme caution dates back to 1878, when Sir John A. Macdonald won re-election as prime minister with what he called his National Policy. It was designed to shelter eastern manufacturers behind lofty tariff walls and to preserve the western Territories as a colony of Eastern Canada. Shedding the stigma of colonialism has preoccupied westerners ever since.

A century ago, the policy probably made sense. At the time of Confederation, the population of the North West Territories (excluding Indians) was about 12,200. Nobody could guess that a million settlers would head west before 1914. Nobody was really prepared to cope with them.

The great migration into the virgin lands was inspired by an enthusiastic colonization campaign by the CPR and the Dominion government. Once built, the railway needed settlers to justify its existence. Neither the railway land nor government land in these parts was worth much without somebody living on it and trying to grow something on it.

This really was the last frontier. Growth in the early days was very slow. Once settlers got to Manitoba, they didn't have much incentive to push on farther west. They had Capt. John Palliser's word for it that a great chunk of the western region was a wilderness, "worthless except here and there."

Calgary's first census was taken in 1884. They counted 428 noses. But somebody cheated, and the figure they published was a grandiose 506. Not much happened during the 1890s. The population was 3,876 in 1891 and 4,091 in 1901 — a gain of only 215 souls.

Calgary had to wait till the 20th century to get moving. Then the census jumped from 11,967 in 1906 to 43,704 in 1911 and 56,514 in 1916. In varying degrees, the same thing was happening everywhere. Towns that weren't on the map one year popped up all over the place the following year.

The shape of things to come was apparent in the district, if not the city itself, as early as 1888, when Calgary-area ranchers shipped 5,000 prime steers to England and the first hail storms were recorded. Hail storms weren't something new. But the fact they were being monitored suggested there now were enough farms in the area for someone to start worrying about them.

Much indignation was aroused when a cowboy found a string of Buck Thorn spiral wire south of the town. Buck Thorn wire was notorious. First used by the railways in the U.S., it was sharp and lanced — the worst kind of barbed wire. For sure now, the open range was gone.

The first more or less permanent settler to put down roots here was a whisky trader, Fred Kanouse. He set up a post seven miles up the Elbow in 1871, thus becoming the first white man to erect anything more permanent than a tent within the present city limits.

His log shack enclosed a living room, store room and trading room. For safety's sake, he had a passage in front admitting Indian customers one at a time. In a few years, however, despite the precautions, he was forced out. His customers were making it known they weren't happy with the arrangement. Kanouse chose to quit rather than fight.

Sam Livingston and John Glenn were more substantial citizens. Both were veterans of the California gold rush. They settled down to farm here in 1875. Livingston planted fruit trees and later brought in the town's first mower, rake, and threshing machine. He raised 14 children and died in 1897. Glenn, situated in Midnapore, grew vegetables and introduced the first irrigation system.

The town's first milk man appeared in 1884. Charlie Jackson owned a buckboard and two five-gallon cans. The milk came from two wild cows owned by Sam Livingston. Jackson had to pin them two falls out of three before he could milk them.

The city has duly enshrined the names of Livingston and Glenn, but in a peculiar sort of way.

John Glenn was a much-respected citizen. He introduced the first irrigation system on his Midnapore farm.

Sam Livingston raised 14 children and a lot of fruit trees. His farm is now the Glenmore Reservoir.

None of the present-day landmarks, it seems, bears any relationship to the actual historic sites.

The Lacombe Home is in Midnapore, where Glenn had his farm. Glenmore Reservoir inundated Livingston's farm, not Glenn's. The Livingston Fish Hatchery, inaugurated in 1973, is on the Pearce Estate, south of the Bow in East Calgary and nowhere near the place where Sam actually tilled the soil.

The Pearce Estate, in turn, was the home of William Pearce, who came to Calgary as superintendent of mines for the North West Territories in 1887. His 15-room mansion, built in 1889, was in its day the town's finest home by far. A giant in his own right, Pearce was a dedicated conservationist who advocated large-scale irrigation long before the CPR actually attempted it.

The CPR launched its colonization and immigration campaign through a subsidiary, the Canada Northwest Land Company. Land was offered at $2.50 an acre, one-sixth in cash, then five annual instalments, and a rebate for working the land.

The rebate was designed to discourage speculators, but it didn't work. Originally aimed at attracting settlers from Europe, particularly Britain, the railway's campaign wound up attracting more Americans than anyone else. And a lot of them were speculators.

Europe still was the first target. Samples of prairie dirt were exhibited in CPR offices overseas. Maps and pamphlets were circulated throughout Europe in English, Welsh, Gaelic, German, French, Dutch, Finnish and Norwegian. Lecturers in Scotland discovered a new device, lantern slides, was ideal for illustrating the joys of life in the Canadian West.

The target countries weren't happy about the prospect of losing their people. They tried to discourage emigration with talk about crop failures, drought and frost. Somehow the CPR managed to get counter-testimonials from 400 farm women saying it wasn't so.

It must have been a confusing time for prospective settlers. They were hearing on the one hand about a Garden of Eden and on the other about a frozen wilderness. Among the disgruntled was an English settler, Charles Carter. In a letter from Calgary to his brother-in-law in London, dated May 1, 1887, he wrote:

"I would not advise any person to leave a good situation in England to come to this country.

"This last winter was a very hard one. The thermometer registered from 20 to 50 below zero for a good part of the time. There were over 10,000 head of cattle froze to death this winter besides sheep and horses and quite a few people as well. And yet they say what a fine country this is.

The winters were harsh and log cabins offered little protection — the scene was 9th Avenue and 8th Street S.E.

A quiet stroll on a hill overlooking the Bow in 1906.

"There are lots of fishing and shooting here. The game consists of mountain sheep, deer, antelope, prairie wolves and foxes, hares, rabbits. There are ducks, geese, teal, widgeon, snipe and prairie chicken which are very fine shooting when they are in season.

"As for myself I have a very bad cold and rheumatism therefore I cannot say I feel well at present. Believe me."

Cecil Denny, who came west with the original Mounties, knew the ropes. In 1895, noting the situation of the new settlers, he penned some advice.

Winters, he assured everybody, were comparatively mild. Farmers could begin plowing in March. Living was cheap. All garden produce and grain could be grown. Hay was plentiful, as was wood for fuel. Farmers should not try to begin in a large way. A few cows, horses, hogs and chickens were enough.

Tyros were warned, too, of other pitfalls to be avoided:

"Keep out of debt. Temperate living is absolutely necessary. Licensed hotels and bars abound and a hard-working farmer coming into town can squander a good portion of his summer's earnings."

A young Ontario farm hand who migrated west in 1889 found Calgarians to be "rather Ontario-English." But he noted also the frequent arrival of carloads of refugees from czarist Russia.

This lad, apparently about 16 years old, worked for a farmer supplying hay to the Mounties. Home was a patch of land beside a slough on Nose Hill. He found the place discomfiting at night, when "we were serenaded, close at hand in the dark, by coyotes — music that at first was alarming to a greenhorn from the east."

Though Calgary lagged a few years behind, the country generally began moving ahead in 1896, when a long period of depression gave way to an era of prosperity that lasted until 1921.

Overseas immigration picked up when the CPR acquired a trans-Atlantic steamship fleet in 1903. There were "home-seekers' excursions" by train from Eastern Canada. Exhibition cars toured the U.S.

The campaign in the U.S. reached as far as Boston. The U.S., which also didn't want to lose its people, launched a counter-propaganda campaign warning that the Canadian winters were cold and

*A tent near the present airport was home for the W. Wright couple (centre)
at the turn of the century.*

British rule was something to be avoided at all costs.

Nevertheless, 9,000 Americans crossed the border in 1898. The exodus reached a peak of 120,000 in 1911. Many of these newcomers were well-to-do. Some were outright speculators, but others simply came looking for better land than what they had in the U.S. They brought money, machinery and livestock with them.

Arrangements were made in advance for settlers arriving from Europe by ship to disembark and go directly to a colonist car. Each newcomer was expected to bring his own luggage and enough food for a five-day journey.

Those who had money could travel in first-class opulence. The railway brass and their friends, mostly politicians, had their own plush private cars. But, for the great majority, the trip west was made in a colonist car.

Passengers sat on hard, slatted seats and likely never knew the reason for the slats was that they made it easier to fumigate the cars between loads.

They slept or tried to sleep, in cumbersome pull-down bunks or on the seats themselves, which also pulled down to form makeshift beds. In the summer, windows were a problem. Leave them closed and the car became hopelessly stuffy. Open them and cinders blew in until everybody was coated with black dust.

A pot-bellied stove was provided for heat, and another stove with an oven so that passengers could warm up soup or milk, make tea or coffee, or even bake bread. Fuel was supplied, but it sometimes ran out and passengers had to forage for wood during stops.

Garlic was popular among many European immigrants. Anyone who didn't like it savored it anyway. Kids ran in the aisles and cried. For single males or harried husbands seeking a respite, each car had a rear smoking area for men only.

It wasn't much by today's standards, but it was a lot better than the covered wagons of the American West. There were no attacks by Indians. That era was gone and forgotten. The chief hazard was prairie fires, started by coals from the engines that often spewed forth and lit up the right of way.

In 1903, the CPR obtained rights to a great block of dry land between Medicine Hat and Calgary. It was the start of a vast irrigation scheme designed to disprove Capt. Palliser's theories about the barren triangle. Headquarters were in Calgary, and the main canal started just a few miles to the east.

In 1906, a railway advertising folder assured everybody that "Alberta has 356 bright, sun-shiny days every year." Maybe that was a misprint and they meant 365 days. When they exaggerated the situation, they normally went all the way.

A newspaper reporter recorded in 1909 that Calgary was prospering, the hotels were crowded, and "the rattle of dice at the cigar counter is unceasing." He left the impression of a wide-open gambling town. Actually they didn't play dice strictly for gambling at that time. A customer would pick up a couple of cigars and roll the proprietor for them, double or nothing.

The town was abuilding with sandstone, and the future was assured. Or was it? No less than 12 families were maintained on relief during the winter. Indignation was expressed in the local press, and "it was openly declared that this sort of thing couldn't go on."

With irrigation available, the CPR was advertising "ready-made farms." If the settler could put up at least $1,500, the company would invest $1,000 to build a house and barn, fence the land, dig a well, and prepare the land for seeding. Again, the principal objective was to encourage immigration from Britain.

In 1911, The Financial Times of London was expressing concern that, in the West, "a good deal of the advantage is passing into American hands.

The American sees for himself and invests. The Englishman is slower to decide."

The Times saw the ready-made farm as the answer. The scheme would "check the Americanization of Western Canada by infusion of a strong and wholesome British strain, attracting so desirable a class that the bad egg is practically unknown."

The Times was wrong on all counts. By 1914 Americans owned most of the ready-made farms. As for bad eggs, remittance men had been giving the yeoman Englishman a bad name for years.

It was a bum rap in many ways. The remittance man, receiving money from home regularly, was seen invariably as a ne'er-do-well son of a "good" family sent out here so he could either kill himself or work out his own regeneration.

All the remittance men were imagined to be cursed with drink, women, or idleness. There was a sort of local pride in telling bigger and better stories about the local remittance man's artics.

Generally overlooked is the fact that many of these characters became mainstays of their respective communities. Well educated and ruggedly independent, they put down roots, worked hard, and made good. If all of them have been tarred with the same brush, it's mainly because the best yarns (or legends) always seemed to centre around the bad eggs.

And some of their exploits were nothing if not imaginative. The story is told of one remittance man whose funds were cut off because he wasn't accomplishing anything. With his bar bill unpaid, he had to do something.

So he borrowed a good horse, hired a fireman in uniform, and had their photo taken in front of the new Calgary courthouse. He sent the photo to England with the explanation that the house was his home, the horse was his own, the uniformed man was his groom, and the land behind the house was his ranch.

His proud parents promptly restored his allowance.

This rowdy child

Looking east on Stephen Avenue in the 1890s.

The familiar rivalry between Edmonton and Calgary goes back a long way. It reached a peak when Edmonton was chosen as the capital of the new province of Alberta in 1905. That hurt. Since then it's been win some, lose some for both sides, and the rivalry continues.

The difference of opinion developed naturally enough. Despite their proximity, the two cities grew up quite differently. Edmonton was a Hudson's Bay post looking north into the muskeg. Calgary was a Mounted Police fort in cow country.

The climate here may have favored the individualist more than the climate up there. Enterprise manifested itself early here in both big ways and small.

The Samuel Shaw family (father, mother, and nine kids from Kent, England) settled in the Fish Creek area in 1883. About the turn of the century, Sam Shaw arranged to have a private telegraph line installed between his farm home and Calgary.

It allowed him to play chess with opponents around the world.

Church men were among the hardiest of the pioneers. Several of them stopped off at Edmonton first, saw the light, and moved to Calgary. Many of the first sandstone buildings here were churches.

How congregations supported them is unclear. It is recorded that the collection plate at the Anglican Church one Sunday contained: 7 bars of soap, 5 mink skins, 1 towel, 1 leather jacket, 1 stone pipe, no money.

The hardships on the frontier were many and varied. Writing home in 1883, an English gentleman grumbled:

"There is no blotting paper in the country, so you need not expect to find that I blotted the last sheet, as I had nothing to blot with."

Some of the amenities of civilization were coming in, however, overland and by rail. Andrew

Bain's Livery Stables on 9th Avenue southeast: a gathering place for horsemen in 1905.

Armour, a printer from Barrie, Ont., and Thomas Braden, a one-time school teacher from Peterborough, set up a Washington hand press in a tent east of the Elbow. The press was shipped in overland, probably via Fort Benton. On Aug. 31, 1883, Armour and Braden published the first edition of The Calgary Herald, Mining and Ranche Advocate and General Advertiser.

The four-page tabloid weekly was an iffy proposition. Gusty, late-summer winds threatened to blow down the tent. Each letter of type had to be set by hand. Subscribers had enlisted for $3 a year, but not everyone was a subscriber. About half the population was illiterate.

The newspaper survived and went on to grow up with the city. Hon. Mackenzie Bowell, then minister of customs, later prime minister, dropped by in September, 1883. Armour and Braden put him to work setting type. About a year later, on Dec. 3,

1884, Hugh St. Quentin Cayley bought the whole operation from the original partners and took over as owner, editor and publisher.

From the earliest days The Herald was embroiled in the issues of the day. An editorial in 1890 complained:

"The inconvenience of receiving only six mails a week from the east was greatly felt this and last week when, owing to snow blockades, the mails have been missing for several days. We understand it is proposed to petition the government to have the full daily mail put on, and the movement will meet with undivided support."

Much progress has been made since then. Snow blockades are no longer a factor, and the town can count on (or at least hope for) five mails a week.

Livery stables were an essential part of any town before the automobile, and Calgary had more than its share. They provided shelter for both horses and transient ranchers, cowboys and farmers. An overnight visitor staggering from one of the bars could always find a hayloft where he could sleep it off.

The stables, mostly downtown, gave the town a distinctive atmosphere. It was blowing in the wind almost all of the time. Nobody noticed it particularly. Everybody was used to it.

A livery stable at 10th Ave. and 2nd St. E. was billed as the biggest barn in Western Canada. Operated by the CPR, it could accommodate 100 teams of horses. By 1910 another outfit, Ruttes Elk Livery, could claim recognition as the city's fanciest barn. It has been described as a sort of apartment house for horses, with ramps for horses with rooms on the upper floor.

The Herald's first home in 1883 on banks of Elbow River. Left to right: an unidentified itinerant preacher; Andrew M. Armour, founder; RCMP Constable Tom Clarke; and Thomas B. Braden, founder.

The first town hall: it was better than meeting in bars.

Calgary's first town council poses for a photographer in 1886: Front row, left to right: Mayor George Murdoch;
Treasurer C. Sparrow; Clerk T. T. A. Boys. Back row: Councillor S. J. Hogg; Assessor J. Campbell;
Solicitor H. Bleeker; Councillor Dr. N. J. Lindsay; Councillor J. H. Millward; Councillor S. J. Clarke;
Chief J. S. Ingram; Collector J. S. Douglas; Councillor I. S. Freeze.

Any self-respecting firm maintained its own stable or at least owned horses and drays. A young man could hire a surrey, with fringe on top, to take a young woman for a ride. Democrats set out daily with loads of land-seekers and helpful realtors promising to show them once-in-a-lifetime opportunities.

One observer summarized early Calgary succinctly as "a great horse town." In 1888, an English reporter writing for The Toronto Globe recorded these impressions:

"I believe that anybody who expressed an opinion derogatory to the past or despairing of the future of the booming little town would be lucky if he escaped with his life. In the streets of Calgary the cowboy at home is met at every turn, and in the hall of the Royal Hotel there are always, day and night, to be seen half-a-dozen genuine ones and half-a-dozen imitation ones."

The reporter noted that "a good many of the cowboys of Calgary are Englishmen by birth" and therefore, naturally, "their fun is generally of a more refined character." With the advent of the Stampede in 1912, the number of imitation cowboys multiplied.

Calgary was incorporated as a town Nov. 17, 1884, and as a city, the first in the North West Territories, Jan. 1, 1894.

Originally there was no local government at all. Even better, there were no taxes. But the first election, in December, 1884, showed that the population was ready to take its politics seriously. There were impassioned speeches and several fist-fights before a council of seven citizens was duly elected and George Murdoch, the harness maker, became the first mayor.

The first town hall was described as "a singular looking wooden structure," high but not very wide. Pictures of it confirm that singular was the word for it. But it was better than nothing. Lacking a town hall, the council had been meeting in bars or anywhere else where the owner of the place would tolerate them.

Having no money to spend, the first council soon ran into financial troubles. Railway time was adopted, but people were having a hard time setting their watches. The solution was to have the Mounties fire their cannon each day at noon. That was a mistake. The Mounties presented the town with a bill for $17.50 for "powder and flannel used in firing the mid-day gun."

The council didn't have $17.50. They had to raise the money through public subscription. The voters may have grumbled about the extravagance, but they came through with the cash. In those days, it was voluntary.

The Mounties at this time weren't too popular. They were the law, period: prosecutors, judge, jury, jailers. When the populace objected, Ottawa responded by providing the town with a stipendiary magistrate, one Jeremiah Travis. His contribution was to make matters worse. An easterner whom nobody liked, Jeremiah sounds like the closest thing to a hanging judge the town ever had.

Among those elected to the first council was former Mountie S. J. Clarke. A rough character, he managed to get into a fight with a Mountie. One account has the Mountie invading Clarke's hotel, looking for illicit booze, and Clarke throwing him out bodily. Whatever happened, Clarke was charged with assaulting a Mountie and "threatening him with a bottle."

Artist John Innes raised the wrath of a judge with his cartoons in The Herald.

In 1894 they knew how to dress for winter: the frontier was backing off; Calgary was a city.

Travis promptly sentenced Clarke to "six months on the woodpile." When the town council objected, Travis declared the recent elections invalid and tossed the council out of office. Such drastic action today might be applauded by many, but in 1884 Jeremiah succeeded only in infuriating the whole town.

The Herald joined the battle with editorials and uncomplimentary cartoons by staff artist John Innes, and an irate Travis reacted by sentencing editor and publisher Hugh St. Q. Cayley to jail for contempt of court.

While never denying that he had a whole lot of contempt for Jeremiah Travis's court, Cayley had to obey the law. Nobody came to arrest him. He was expected to deliver himself to the Mounties' jail. He obliged, and it was an occasion to remember.

On a cold December night, Hugh Cayley was escorted to the barracks in a wagon accompanied by a brass band and torchlight procession. Along

the way the editor delivered impromptu orations on the freedom of the press. At each bar everybody stopped "to thaw out the band's instruments."

Artist John Innes (no relation to today's staff artist, Tom Innes) reflected that Travis was "a good enough fellow in his way, but he never got in tune with the West."

Innes never went to jail and Cayley's stay there was brief. He was released, and another procession brought him home. Everything sorted itself out when Judge Travis was assigned elsewhere, another election was held and G. C. King, the Mountie who first forded the Bow River, became the town's second mayor.

The town survived the Travis incident with high good humor but lost its cool altogether in 1885, when the Second Riel Rebellion threatened to reverse the fragile new balance of power in the West.

Fifty-five Calgary Mounties headed east to help put out the fire. That left seven Mounties in the Calgary garrison. Out there somewhere were about 3,000 Indians who weren't sure whose side they were on. The town didn't much like the odds, and there was much shouting and running about.

District rancher Tom Strange, a former military man, rounded up a local army of cowboys, homesteaders, bank tellers and clerks. They, too, went off to fight the war. Then Strange went back to ranching. Once more Crowfoot held his people in check, and Calgary escaped unscathed.

The frontier backed off a bit farther on July 21, 1890, when the first sod was turned for the Calgary-Edmonton Railway. A general holiday was proclaimed. Everybody turned out to celebrate.

They barbecued an ox and washed it down with champagne and beer. There was a parade of 150 carriages. While they were at it, they inaugurated the town waterworks.

Edmonton was no luckier than Calgary when it came to getting the tracks where they wanted them. The line ran to Strathcona (now South Edmonton) and stopped. Unlike Calgary, Edmonton refused to move the town to the railway depot. In due course,

a bridge was built across the North Saskatchewan River.

Weeds were a hazard on the Edmonton run. In the summer they grew so high they would stop the train. The foliage "greased" the track, and the engine's wheels just spun around. While the train crew cut down the weeds, the passengers got out to pick flowers, toss rocks, or just browse around the countryside.

In 1890, the Calgary town council passed bylaws prohibiting the firing of revolvers on main streets and the grazing of cattle on Stephen (now 8th) Ave.

The turn of the century found Calgary with a population of about 4,000. Males outnumbered females three to one. A sea serpent was sighted in the Bow River. Men's fashions stressed bowler hats, wing collars and checked suits.

The big event of 1901 was an official visit by the lieutenant-governor, premier, and members of the Territorial Legislature.

People painted their houses so the visitors would be impressed. When paint ran short, they

Stephen Avenue in the 1880s when Calgary was "a great horse town".

Calgary's skyline maintained a low profile in 1906, but Alberta was only a year old.

just painted the front. But the visiting dignitaries arrived late, at about 3 a.m. Much to his chagrin, Mayor J. S. Mackie discovered the next morning they were in town and he had missed meeting them. He ordered everybody back to the CPR depot so he could read his speech.

There was a parade and banquet. As a special privilege, the ladies were allowed to sit on a balcony and watch the men eat. Women didn't have the vote. Nor did they eat with the men on state occasions.

Inspecting A. E. Cross's Calgary Brewery, the visitors overstayed their welcome outrageously. Part of the rest of their schedule had to be scrapped so they could be poured back onto their train, presumably happy and dully impressed with the North West Territories' first city.

The city's accelerating growth produced a scandal in 1904. Five hundred lots were put up for sale. Buyers who turned up in the morning found the best lots had been sold overnight. Some aldermen and their friends had grabbed them, it was charged. The most indignant protestor was an alderman who thought he had a piece of the action but didn't get anything.

An inquiry concluded that there had been "gross carelessness" on the part of the mayor and council. Two aldermen, the city solicitor, the city clerk and an auditor resigned. As historian J. W. Grant MacEwan has noted, "The waters in

Calgary's civic sea have never remained calm for long."

On Sept. 1, 1905, Alberta and Saskatchewan became provinces, carved out of the North West Territories. Regina, capital of the Territories, became the capital of Saskatchewan. In Alberta everybody got into the act. Red Deer and Banff put in a bid, as did other communities, but Calgary and Edmonton were the chief contenders.

Calgary sent a delegation to Ottawa. So did Edmonton. Edmonton was chosen as the "provisional" capital, and the final decision was left to the new Alberta Legislature. The Legislature voted for Edmonton, 16 to 8.

Having failed to get the capital, Calgary figured it should at least get the university. A fine site was chosen west of town. Promoters subdivided the land and sold 25-foot lots away out on top of a hill in the middle of nowhere. They called it Varsity Heights.

But Edmonton got the university, too, and Calgary had to wait a long time for a campus to call its own.

Twice defeated, the foothills city could only fall back on the reassuring reality of a continuing boom. Boosters were able to record in 1909 that industrial Calgary now embraced 97 wholesale warehouses plus factories producing biscuits, soap, candy, breakfast food, coffee, spice, and macaroni. There were two steam laundries.

Next page: The horse-and-buggy days added a touch of glamor to the twilight of the last century. In 1893 Bob Hodgson paused in his carriage for this memorable photograph in front of the Alexander Allan home on Angus Avenue, now 6th Avenue.

The sandstone city

City Hall, shortly after opening.

Growth, to many, has become a dirty six-letter word. Statistics Canada persists in singling out Calgary as the fastest-growing city in Canada. Many Calgarians, it has been suggested, would be glad to give up the honor, for a little while at least, just so they could catch their breath. It isn't an unmitigated blessing.

In the early days there were no qualms about growth. Boosterism was a way of life. The favorite boast was that the city was becoming "another Chicago." Happily for all concerned, it never quite came to that.

The changing pattern of life was noted by The Calgary Herald as early as Sept. 3, 1884, when an editorial stated, unequivocibly, that "the free and easy life of the old frontiersman has departed." Long processions of "halfbreed carts or the ox-teams dragging their weary feet amid a profusion of oaths and western slang" had given way to "the polite demeanor of the Pullman car."

The musical talent of the city was evident for all to see and hear at public and private concerts. The medical and legal fraternities were well represented, whereas "two years ago not a single member of either profession was to be found in our embryo city."

The first permanent townsite grew out of the bald prairie north of the CPR tracks. The railroad offered choice lots for sale in December, 1883. To eliminate jostling and shoving at the land office, names of the would-be buyers were drawn from a hat.

Appropriately, pioneer settler John Glenn drew the No. 1 ticket. The price of each lot was about $200, and Glenn bought two of them. If he had lived, he would have wound up with corner lots at 9th Ave. and Centre St. and at 8th Ave. and 2nd St. S.W.

Newcomer James Lougheed bought up every lot he could get his hands on. It seemed like a good way to go broke. The way it worked out, he knew what he was doing. The lots he bought in time were found to be located on 7th and 8th Aves. in downtown Calgary.

At first all the streets and avenues had names, not numbers. Unlike so many other communities, Calgary never had a Main Street. The town is almost unique in that respect. Here are the streets and avenues as they originally were designated:

South from the river, the avenues were Abbott (2nd), Egan (3rd), Reinach (4th), Northcote (5th), Angus (6th), McIntyre (7th), Stephen (8th) and Atlantic (9th). East to west, the streets were Drinkwater (2nd E.), Osler (1st E.), McTavish (Centre), Scarth (1st W.) and Hamilton (2nd W.).

Father Lacombe's mission away up the Elbow River was considered to be so far out of town it didn't count. The present commercial and residential district around 17th Ave. and 14th St. S.W. would remain a cattle ranch for many years to come.

When, in 1904, they changed all the names to numbers, not much of historical value was lost. Most of the names belonged to CPR officials, then-prominent townspeople, or officers of the Mounted Police. The CPR's George Stephen became Lord Mount Stephen, which he likely prized more highly than an avenue out here.

The shack-town that grew up along the new thoroughfares looked like something waiting to either burn down or fall down. As it happened, it burned down before it fell down. This was traditional in all western communities, wherever they were. They all, at one time or another, had their Great Fire.

Calgary's Great Fire occurred on a Sunday morning, Nov. 7, 1886. It began in a log structure, the local bucket brigade couldn't cope with it, and 14 buildings were lost, including four stores, three warehouses, three hotels, a tinsmith shop and, worst of all, a saloon. Volunteers saved a few buildings by pulling down George Murdoch's harness shop.

Surveying the valuable real estate so unexpectedly made available for immediate urban renewal, the town made a fateful decision. Some shacks would be rebuilt, of course, but henceforth

Hudson's Bay store in 1891.

Calgary was to be distinguished among all prairie communities as the Sandstone City.

Prior to the Great Fire, the main structures consisted of logs and milled lumber. The lumber came from James Walker's saw mill. Prior to that, except for the original log buildings, practically everything was under canvas. The Herald wasn't the only business to start in a tent. The first hotels were tents.

The impact of sandstone after 1886 is summed up by the Alberta Historical Society in a booklet entitled *Calgary in Sandstone:*

"Calgary could have developed like other prairie towns, with frame buildings lining the streets, interspersed here and there by the brick structures of successful businessmen. Instead, the existence of stone quarries enabled Calgary to become a solid substantial

Calgary begins to show class: the Mount Royal area in 1911.

A few Calgarians were able to live in a grand manner. Top photo shows the residence of Senator James Lougheed. Located on 13th Ave. S.W., it was known as "Beaulieu". In the bottom photo is the home of William Roper Hull, built in 1905 at the corner of 12th Ave. and 6th Street S.W.

A construction crew at work on the Central Methodist Church in 1907.

William Roper Hull in the early 1900s. He believed a man's home should be a castle.

William Pearce's mansion at 2014, 17th Ave. S.E. It was torn down in 1957.

The scene on Atlantic Ave. (9th) east of Centre Street after the 1886 fire.

town, compared by promoters to the successful American city of Denver, Colo."

Regardless of the worth of such comparisons, the unique character of the city, as reflected by its remaining sandstone buildings, is still there for anyone who wants to go looking for it.

Surviving old-timers built in the downtown sector between 1888 and 1912 include Alberta Corner (formerly the Alberta Hotel), the Grain Exchange Building, City Hall, the Church of the Redeemer, Central United Church, Knox Presbyterian Church and the Salvation Army Citadel.

There are many others along the 8th Ave. mall, but many are half-hidden behind neon signs. Their sandstone origins are more evident from the back lanes. It's estimated there still are about 40 sandstone buildings between the river and 19th Ave. S.W. and about an equal number scattered about the rest of the city.

The first courthouse, built in 1888 on 4th St. near 7th Ave. S.W., is gone, but the second, built in 1912 on 7th Ave. near 5th St. S.W., still was occupied in 1974 by the Glenbow-Alberta Museum. In 1909, the six-storey Grain Exchange Building at 9th Ave. and 1st St. S.W. qualified as Calgary's first skyscraper.

The Hudson's Bay Company bought out I. G. Baker in 1891 and occupied a sandstone store at the northwest corner of 8th Ave. and Centre St. until 1929, when they moved the whole business to 7th Ave. and 1st St. S.W.

Before 1900, when dikes were built, the Bow River overflowed every spring, which was distracting for anyone living on Abbott, Egan, Reinach or Northcote. Some of the city's finest first homes were on Reinach (4th) Ave. So they wouldn't float away every spring, the plank sidewalks on Reinach and Northcote were wired together.

Ushering in the sandstone era, Wesley F. Orr and Joseph Butlin were operating sandstone quarries in the mid-1800s. Butlin, a former Mountie, took up ranching 2½ miles up the Elbow River in 1880, but his chief asset wasn't cows. An 1885 directory described a more significant natural resource:

"For a distance of 300 yards on the exposed bank a seam of splendid freestone about six feet in depth crops out. The distance to the CPR line is only two miles, and as the quarry is to be worked by enterprising capitalists, a spur line can easily be constructed."

Other early quarries were operated by Thomas Edworthy in the Shaganappi district near the Banff Coach Road and by Col. Barwis and John McCallum north of the Bow River near Prince's Island.

In 1896 John McCallum, proprietor of Sunny Side Quarry, sent a sandstone bassinette, so large it required a railway flat car to haul it, to the Chicago World's Fair. It won a medallion.

Original stone cliffs still can be seen near the intersection of the Sarcee Trail and Banff Coach

Road, but most of the original sites are long lost, buried under roads and residences. They were situated on both sides of the Bow, the Elbow, and Nose Creek, and as far away as Cochrane and Okotoks. Sandstone from a quarry near Cochrane was used to build the Legislative Building in Edmonton.

The sandstone era lasted about 30 years and ended with the introduction of brick, limestone, and other types of building stone. At the peak of the sandstone era, it was estimated that half the working population of Calgary consisted of stone masons.

Brickburn today is a dot on the map along the CPR main line, south of the Bow River, north of the CFCN television tower, and about a mile inside the city limits. In its day it was a community separate from Calgary, with its own post office.

Crandall Pressed Brick and Sandstone Company bought 400 acres at Brickburn in 1905 and employed 100 men cutting stone and making bricks. A village sprang up with houses for married couples, boarding houses, a church, and some shops. The community survived with its own identity until the Depression.

Crandall, of Crandall Pressed Brick and so on, built his own home of brick from Brickburn along the northeastern side of Varsity Heights. Though the town didn't survive, the house did. Today it's occupied by wrestling promoter Stu Hart, his wife Helen, their large family, and various itinerant practitioners of the manly art of grunt 'n groan.

The builders of the sandstone era were free spirits who worked each stone with loving care and let their imaginations run free. Contemplating the scene about 1915, a visiting architect was at a loss to categorize it. He would end up calling it "typical Calgary."

He found that Gothic, Renaissance, classical and the French Second Empire "all found some expression." Commercial buildings had a "massive" look about them. But the style wasn't rigid. Various buildings combined exterior decoration, towers, bays, wall projections and recesses with a fine disregard for continuity.

City Hall amply demonstrates the durability of sandstone. The corner stone was laid in 1907, and the building was officially opened in 1911. It's still there, withstanding cold winter winds outside and heated internally by gusts of hot air.

Among the first builders of big sandstone buildings it was only natural that James A. Lougheed, Calgary's first lawyer, first senator, and first Albertan to be knighted, played a prominent role. From the time of the first CPR sale, he had made a point of buying up all the land that nobody else wanted.

The Lougheed Building, at 6th Ave. and 1st St. S.W., was built in 1911. His other buildings are readily identifiable. He named them after his sons: Clarence, Edgar, Douglas, Norman. He was 35 years old when he was appointed to the Senate by Sir John A. Macdonald in 1889.

The Hull Opera House when it was the focal point of Calgary society.

Looking for a partner, Senator Lougheed heard about a bright young lawyer in New Brunswick and brought R. B. Bennett out here. Bennett became prime minister of Canada in 1930. Peter Lougheed, the senator's grandson, became premier of Alberta in 1971.

The first Lougheed home in Calgary, built in 1884, was a comparatively modest frame house, but it did have a distinctive touch — bay windows imported from Ontario. The Three Greenhorns restaurant occupies the site today at 4th St. and 4th Ave. S.W.

Beaulieu, the Lougheed sandstone mansion built in 1892 at 13th Ave. and 6th St. S.W., still stands. Visitors are welcome, but come prepared to give blood. Renovated and expanded, it's now the Red Cross blood donor clinic.

The Lougheed mansion overlooked an ornate fountain and landscaped terraces sloping away to the east. The garden today is occupied by a small apartment building appropriately named The Senator. Once, the beautiful people of Calgary gathered there under the summer sun to take tea. Edward, Prince of Wales, was an occasional visitor, though he preferred his own EP Ranch west of High River.

A Lougheed neighbor who also believed a man's home should be a castle was William Roper Hull. The Hull mansion at 12th Ave. and 6th St. S.W. was equipped for any eventuality. Since the fuel supply was a doubtful proposition, the kitchen stoves were geared for wood or coal, gas, or electricity.

Eric L. Harvie, Q.C., bought the Hull Estate in 1955, and for several years it was headquarters for the Glenbow Foundation. Now only the name is left. The Hull Estate is an immense apartment block.

W. R. Hull, originally a rancher and later a builder, gave his name to the Hull Opera House at 6th Ave. and Centre St. For a time it was the only amusement centre in town. Now it's only a long-gone memory. Pending another skyscraper, the site is a parking lot.

Built in 1893, the Hull Opera House enjoyed its cultural heyday from 1893 to about 1906. The early townspeople used to hold "amateur theatricals" in their homes. The idea sounds positively stifling, but these amateurs must have had something going for them. In time they were competing on the Opera House stage with touring professional companies.

Among those jostling for space on the boards were the Calgary Amateur Dramatic Club and the Calgary Opera Company. The former offered songs, sketches and "screaming" farces, the latter favored Gilbert and Sullivan. In winter audiences at the Hull Opera House, dressed to the nines in glittering gowns, long white kid gloves and white ties and tails, got to and from the theatre in horse-drawn sleighs. In 1900-1901, they tossed coins onto the stage in aid of veterans of the Boer War.

William Pearce's 15-room mansion in East Calgary survived until 1957. He called it Bowbend Shack. Some shack: it had a billiard room in the basement, bathroom with running water and toilet, three fireplaces, hardwood floors, elaborate panelling, and black walnut pillars guarding the entrance.

A sandstone General Hospital (later Rundle Lodge) was built beside the Elbow River in 1894. The site today is 12th Ave. and 6th St. S.E. In 1894 it was away out in the middle of nowhere. A winding dirt trail ran from the city to the hospital building. The only neighboring structure was a little frame clubhouse, home of the city's first golf course on the Elbow River flats.

On Sept. 2, 1907, the Workers of the World (Calgary branch) turned out on parade. Prominent among them, and justly proud of their contribution, were the stone masons and cutters. A newspaper account noted that:

"A monstrous stone, measuring several yards long, the work of the quarrymen, received a cheer from the crowds. This received third prize and was well won. Six horses were required to drag it along."

It's the only time on record that a big stone won a prize in a Calgary parade. But it was fitting. Stone was the raw material that transformed the struggling community of tents and shacks into something unique, solid, and permanent.

Beds and bars

Calgary House: "a model of taste".

A lot of the old-timers are gone — the Blue Rock, the Empire, the Yale, the Royal, the Wales and the old Noble. One minute they're there, it seems, and the next minute they're gone. On Sunday morning, March 17, 1974, demolition crews detonated dynamite in the basement of the Wales Hotel at 7th Ave. and 2nd St. S.W. In a matter of seconds a proud old hostelry was reduced to rubble. It can happen that fast.

When a hotel closes, the regulars gather to drink a toast and shed a tear. Then only the memories remain, embellished with the passing of time until no one is really quite sure where fact ends and fancy begins.

It's accepted as historic fact that the longest bar in the West in the old days was the 125-footer in the Alberta Hotel. But L. R. Seymour, 85 years old in 1973, worked as a desk clerk in the Alberta Hotel from 1911 to 1915, and he remembers that the longest bar was down the street in the old Royal Hotel. And he should know. He was there.

The Royal was a three-storey building at 8th Ave. and Centre St. Guests occupying the top floor were divided by cotton partitions, males on one side, females on the other, though the clientelle in this establishment was predominantly male in any case.

The longest bar stretched from the street to the lane. That a bar of such dimensions was physically possible can be can be verified today. The distance from the street to the lane is 130 feet. To keep the drinks flowing from one end to the other, the Royal employed four bartenders on each shift.

Whether any other city in the West realistically could claim a longer bar is open to conjecture. In any case, the Royal had another claim to fame. Its owner, Charlie Bell, was celebrated as the greatest champagne drinker west of the Great Lakes. His intake was six pints a day at least, and he often did better than that.

The Alberta Hotel in its day qualified as the No. 1 hotel in town, not because of the length of its bar but because it was the classiest spot in town and attracted the best clientelle. In some ways the place could be called grubby by today's standards, but other lodgings were grubbier and the Alberta Hotel's place in history is secure.

Built in 1888-89, the Alberta survived as a hotel until Prohibition put it out of business in 1916. H. A. Perley was the first manager, succeeded by Norman Jackson, then Charles Taprell from 1908 to 1916, when they converted it into a combined retail and office building.

Credit Stewart Green Properties Ltd. for the fact the sandstone building that housed the Alberta Hotel still occupies the southeast corner of 8th Ave. and 1st St. S.W.

The theory is that all the old buildings don't have to be torn down. Some can be restored. The Alberta Block isn't a hotel any more, but, after sand-blasting and a good washing down, the old landmark looks today much the same as it did in the 1890s.

The Alberta Hotel wasn't Calgary's first hostelry. A vintage picture of Calgary House, built at the east end of town during construction of the CPR, shows something that, charitably, can only be called less than lavish. It's a sorry-looking sight, but the first edition of The Calgary Herald, Aug. 31, 1883, nevertheless gave the shack a rave review:

"We have had the pleasure of inspecting the new hotel just completed by Dunne and Wright, and find it a perfect model of taste and neatness. It contains a large comfortable parlor, and a number of bed-rooms, all handsomely carpeted and furnished in the best of style.

"The dining-room has accommodation for about 40 guests and the reading room is well supplied with the latest papers. Messrs. Dunne & Wright are well and favorably known to the public, and we have no doubt they will receive the large share of public patronage which they so justly inherit."

Lists of rules supposedly posted by various hotels in the 1880s indicate that guests didn't expect to be pampered. These lists are all suspiciously similar, suggesting they could be the figment of someone's imagination. A guest checking into a

The Royal Hotel: four bartenders were needed to handle its long bar.

The bar at the King Edward. In the centre, Louis Charlebois, proprietor.

hotel allegedly could expect to be admonished as follows:

1. Guests will be provided with breakfast and supper but must rustle their own dinner.

2. Boots and spurs must be removed at night before retiring.

3. Dogs are not allowed in the bunks but may sleep underneath.

4. Candles, hot water and other luxuries charged extra, also soap.

5. Two or more persons must sleep in one bed when so requested by the proprietor.

6. The proprietor will not be responsible for anything. In case of fire, guests are requested to escape without unnecessary delay.

7. All guests are requested to rise at 6 a.m. This is imperative as sheets may be needed for tablecloths.

8. Tips are to be left with the proprietor, who will distribute them to the staff if considered necessary.

9. When guests find themselves or their baggage thrown over the fence, they may consider that they have received notice to quit.

10. Guests will bury their own dead.

Kamoose Taylor, who ran a hotel in Fort Macleod, purportedly had such a list of rules. But a tourist today can find a similar list in a frontier village near Reno, Nevada. This kind of coincidence tends to cast doubt on the veracity of the whole business.

To the extent that such rules may have, in part, reflected actual conditions, places like the Alberta Hotel certainly would have qualified as luxurious.

While restoring the Alberta Block, Stewart Green discovered various oddities. The inside of the building is hollow, an arrangement that permitted each room to receive natural light. Often, that was the only kind of light obtainable. Advertisements for hotels frequently stressed that "every room has lots of daylight."

Bumping about in the morning, the guest would appreciate any convenience he could get. Most rooms came equipped with only jugs and basins. Anyone wanting hot water had to run downstairs for it.

From the time it opened with a "citizens dinner" to celebrate the occasion until 1914, when the Palliser opened and dwarfed everything else in town, the Alberta Hotel was the only hotel that justifiably could be designated as "modern." It had such amenities as a good (though not huge) bar, a dining room and barber shop, and reasonably comfortable rooms upstairs.

Old photographs show that the place had a lived-in look. They show a big lobby with a good-sized staircase and big leather chairs stuffed with horse hair and dented wherever anyone had sat in them.

The chairs in the lobby were well used since there were none in the bar. Customers stood in the bar as long as they could, then repaired to the lobby and sat there until they got thirsty again. The bar and the dining room were on the main floor, the barber shop downstairs.

The Alberta Hotel on the southeast corner of 8th Ave. and 1st St. S.W.

The Alberta Hotel's famed "longest bar" which actually wasn't.

Barber shops were essential to the social and business life of the early community. Coffee breaks were unknown. Instead, the men of the town would assemble in the barber shop for a leisurely shave or whatever. It was an excellent opportunity to mull over and assess the events of the day while contemplating the future.

An old-time bellhop at the Alberta Hotel recorded how his duties included keeping the fire going in the stove in the lobby and putting out fires in the mattresses in the bedrooms. On cold winter evenings, guests gathered around the stove in the lobby "to expound and expectorate."

Cattle barons Pat Burns and George Lane maintained upstairs rooms year-round. They expected water to be delivered to them every morning, even when the pipes were frozen.

The story is told of a remittance man who, dead drunk, rode into the bar on a black horse, shooting his pistol indiscriminately. The management calmly presented him with a bill for $2,800 to replace broken mirrors, bottles and glasses. He paid it.

Then there is the tale of the tall, dark stranger who stepped up to bartender Tom Pierce, took a revolver out of his pocket, and placed it on the counter. His intent was armed robbery. But Pierce just lifted a soda siphon up to eye level and pumped "a big charge" into the would-be holdup man's face. He stumbled out empty handed.

Most early hotels opened early and offered the first drink free to all customers arriving between 6 and 9 a.m. The trick, of course, was to make the rounds, picking up free drinks and thereby getting the day off to a hilarious start.

Though the Alberta and the Royal were on 8th Ave., most of the first hotels were on 9th Ave. A strategic location was important, and a location opposite the railway tracks was strategic.

The Atlantic Hotel, at the east end of Atlantic (9th) Ave., was known fondly as "the Bucket of Blood." The name commemorated a shooting escapade that occurred there. In this case, it is said, someone actually got killed. If there was a police record of it, it's long lost. The police were notoriously careless about keeping records about anything.

Though it had a reputation as a rough, tough place, the Atlantic, built in 1890, originally was a temperance house. The temperance idea was dis-

In 1912, the Grand Union Hotel on 9th Ave. S.E. was doing a thriving business.

Grand Union Hotel, Calgary.

carded in 1896 when the house got a licence to serve liquor. For anyone travelling east, the Atlantic became the "Last Chance Saloon." There was nothing beyond it except open prairie.

The Blue Rock Hotel was the "Last Chance Saloon" for anyone travelling south. This two-storey frame building, located east of the present Mission Bridge, originally was the home of the Calgary Pigeon Shooting Club. When the club got a liquor licence, the pigeon shooters moved out and two-fisted drinkers moved in.

The idea of "Last Chance" bars in every direction leading out of town suggests everybody was incapable of leaving town until he had been adequately refreshed. For those coming into town, Last Chance bars doubled as First Chance bars. Either way, it was wet.

The Empress Hotel, on 6th Ave., opened in 1911. It was noteworthy mainly because it boasted a grand total of four bathrooms for each 22-room floor. The original Noble Hotel, on 1st St. S.W., opened in 1912. Its chief claim to fame was the city's first elevator.

If one hotel, aside from the Alberta, characterizes Calgary, it would be the Shamrock, in east Calgary at 2101 11th St. S.E. Built in 1918 and extensively refurbished in 1971, "The Rock" is in a class by itself. Where else would they serve green beer on St. Patrick's Day? Where else would the customers drink it?

The original quality of the Shamrock Hotel stems to a large extent from its location. A railway line runs right past the front door. Beyond are the stockyards, packing plants, and some lumber yards. For those who work in the area the Shamrock is an informal club, not just another pub.

This corner of town quite possibly reflects what Calgary really is more than any other corner. Bring together the stockyards, the packing plants, and a rail line, and it's a big chunk of instant history. Here, at least, the character of old Calgary hasn't changed all that much.

More trucks than trains rumble past the front door now, but through the era of the big steam engines no one staying in the hotel portion of the Shamrock ever complained about the noise. They were used to it. If it had stopped they probably would have sat up in bed wide awake, wondering what happened.

Folklore has it that years ago workers at the Burns packing plant had a tunnel enabling them to escape to the Shamrock beer parlor. The foreman would look around the plant and notice that the afternoon shift seemed pretty thin. He never figured out how everybody got past the timekeeper.

Today, brash newcomers like the Calgary Inn, the International and the Four Seasons loom large downtown, and others reach out into the suburbs. They are hotels, motels, or motor hotels; clean, shiny and new, with vibrating beds, color tv and dark, polished bars.

The Palliser, while retaining some of its old-time flavor, has been extensively renovated. The Shamrock and a few others are still in business, and oft-told tales still commemorate their uniquely individual traditions.

Front page thunderer

Bob Edwards, owner, editor and publisher of The Calgary Eye-Opener, was a man among men, a character among characters, and the social conscience of the city. Anyone looking for the prototypical Calgarian would have to stop and take a long look at Mr. Edwards.

In a world grown more cynical than it ever was in his day, the question is asked whether the facts about Bob Edwards really support the legend. Happily, the answer is yes, they do. Bob Edwards never apologized for anything. Nobody needs to apologize for him.

Author W. O. Mitchell, who has a keen eye for what's sham and what's real, harbors no reservations about Edwards:

"He commented so well on the style and customs of his day. It was natural for him to become a legend, but the legend isn't too far from what he actually was. Edwards, like the Mounties, represents the real thing. They really did exist, they grew right out of the soil and history of the country."

Neither the original Mounties nor the editor of The Eye-Opener was born here, and both possessed their share of all-too-human flaws. But their accomplishments (the Mounties in establishing the city, Bob Edwards in defining it) far outweigh the flaws. They are more secure than mere folklore ever could make them.

Grant MacEwan, whose books include a biography called *Eye-Opener Bob*, says of Bob Edwards:

"He exerted a public influence which probably surpassed that of any western editorial or political figure of his time."

Robert Chambers Edwards: sketch by R. Randolph Bruce.

In a six-part feature in The Herald in 1956, former Herald associate editor Andrew Snaddon, now editor of The Edmonton Journal, said of Bob Edwards:

"He carried Calgary's fame far and wide long before Social Credit put oil in the ground or Mayor Mackay ever gave away a white hat. Bob and Calgary went together."

Much later, in 1970, columnist George Bain wrote in The Toronto Globe and Mail that The Eye-Opener, like the city, was in its time witty, scandalous, irreverent, daft — and socially aware. Agreeing that Bob Edwards reflected the community where he lived, Bain commented:

"Any community that provided a congenial climate for a Bob Edwards — he couldn't abide Toronto, for instance, and found little enough to detain him in Winnipeg — couldn't be all bad. Neither, of course, could it be all good."

Here is Edwards' own comment on the city shortly after he moved here:

"Picturesquely situated so as to be within easy reach of the brewery, Calgary extends right and left, north and south, up and down, in and out, expanding as she goes, swelling in her pride, puffing in her might, blowing in her majesty and revolving in eccentric orbits round a couple of dozen large bars which close promptly at 11:30 right or wrong."

Robert Chambers Edwards, born in Edinburgh Sept. 12, 1864, travelled widely before arriving here via Texas, Wetaskiwin, Leduc, and High River. He abandoned Calgary at one point to test the climate in Ontario and Manitoba. As George Bain noted, he never found those places to his liking.

If he found Calgary congenial, he also helped shape it in his own image. He refused ever to let the place get too stuffy or take itself too seriously.

His caustic wit and earthy humor deflated the high and mighty. Fearless, eloquent and witty in print, he was quiet and retiring in person. He drank far too much, to the point where he often knocked both himself and his newspaper out of circulation — then in 1915 he supported prohibition.

The first Eye-Opener was published in High River March 4, 1902. But the editor didn't stay there long. The popular story of how he came to leave has to do with a gramaphone salesman and the local church.

This salesman arrived in town trying to convince the church that it should employ recorded music in place of its off-key choir. He set up a demonstration. It went well until, apparently, some culprit switched the records. Expecting to hear Nearer My God to Thee, the congregation instead got a rousing rendition of Just Because She Made Them Goo-Goo Eyes. Edwards denied responsibility, but everybody blamed him anyway.

Celebrated lawyer Paddy Nolan happened to be in High River to defend a cattle rustler. He induced Edwards to move to Calgary. And High River's loss was Calgary's everlasting gain.

Fittingly enough, Edwards' first home here was a room in the Alberta Hotel. In the years to come, with time out to dry out, often in a hospital, he was a near-permanent patron of the Alberta bar.

Lawyer Paddy Nolan persuaded Bob Edwards to move to Calgary. This portrait was taken around 1910.

Though they spread their business around, the Alberta remained the favorite watering hole for Edwards, Nolan and their cohorts, including many of the era's most prosperous ranchers.

That The Eye-Opener ever amounted to anything at all is remarkable when you consider that Edwards' office consisted of one room, in which he worked at a roll-top desk; the paper, supposedly a weekly, appeared whenever he felt like putting it out; he had no printing plant, relying instead on the plants of other newspapers; he had no subscription list, no ledger — and, really, no news.

The Eye-Opener offered mainly comment and opinion. The saving grace was the superb quality of both.

Edwards' observations were mild enough in the beginning. "Although the citizens of Calgary. are not what you would call violently insane," he remarked, "they still indulge in picnics to an alarming extent, eating sand and ants and doing other things which we admit are mildly idiotic."

Before long he was taking aim at bigger targets. A champion of the underdog, he soon discerned that the top dog in these parts was the CPR. In particular he didn't like the way in which the CPR was dilly-dallying about providing safe railway crossings. This straight-faced report appeared in The Eye-Opener in 1906:

"Not a life was lost or a buggy smashed at the CPR crossing last week."

Unappreciative of such compliments, the CPR banned The Eye-Opener from all its transcontinental trains.

Edwards responded by running a series of pictures of spectacular train wrecks. It didn't matter where the wrecks occurred, or on what line. Each bore the caption, *"Another CPR Wreck."* Edwards' coup de grace was a large picture of R. B. Bennett, the sober-sided counsel for the CPR. The caption was the same: *"Another CPR Wreck."*

The railway capitulated. The Eye-Opener was readmitted for sale on the cross-country trains.

Bob Edwards published The Eye-Opener out of Calgary, off and on, from 1903 until 1922. Andrew. Snaddon related how it was still a young, mostly single men's country, full of drifters and speculators, a land of boom and bust. Edwards was very much at home with everybody except the pompous and frivolous.

Bob Edwards: 1864-1922.

His prose was sometimes bawdy but rarely crude. He could be irreverent when the need arose. Overly-pompous church men were a favorite target. In The Eye-Opener, the WCTU was the Women's Continual Temperance Uproar.

Some of the "better" people pretended they never read The Eye-Opener. They paid a quarter to have it smuggled into their homes. The price on the street was five cents a copy or $1 a year.

"It should be $10 a year," Edwards complained, "but due to the irregularity of its appearance and the occasional punk issue, we just charge one buck."

Personally, Bob Edwards wasn't a flamboyant character. He favored grey suits and christie hats. He was always "well dressed and well pressed." Though short and stocky, he had a distinguished look about him. He was well educated. Usually he held his liquor well, but not always. On those occasions when the Demon Rum overcame him, he

Eye Opener front page, Oct. 5, 1908. Edwards was "editor and proprietor".

was the first to admit it as soon as he was up and about again and able to publish another paper.

The best resume of his philosophy was written by Bob Edwards himself. It is contained in a prayer that occasionally ran at the head of his news columns. Here it is in its entirety:

"Lord, let me keep a straight path in the presence of solemn asses; let me not truckle to the high or bulldoze the low; let me frolic with the Jack and Joker, and win the game; lead me unto truth and beauty and tell me her name; keep me sane, but not too sane; let me con-

demn no man because of his grammar and no woman because of her morals, neither being responsible for either.

"Preserve my sense of humor and values and proportions. Let me be healthy while I live but not live too long. Which is about all for today, Lord. Amen."

To help deflate any who had lost their sense of humor and values and proportions, he introduced a most singular column of "Society Notes." Typical entries:

Edwards' town: Calgary's 8th Ave., looking west, in 1911.

"Maude De Vere of Drumheller arrived in the city Wednesday afternoon and was run out of town Wednesday night. It is a pity Miss De Vere is not a race horse. She is very fast."

"Miss Jessie Marshfield is staying in Banff for a few days nursing her alleged father, whose addiction to whisky is most distressing to his friends, especially as he seldom has the price."

He invented mythical characters who turned up so often in the pages of The Eye-Opener that they threatened at times to become more celebrated than Bob Edwards himself. The best-known pair were Peter McGonigle, cattle thief and editor of The Midnapore Gazette, and Albert (Bertie) Buzzard-Cholomondley, of Skookingham Hall, Skookingham, Hants, England, a remittance man constantly in need of funds.

Though the names might be fictional, the antics of Edwards' characters frequently were familiar enough to make some real characters uncomfortable. Whatever name Edwards used, readers readily identified the subject. Anyone on the receiving end was guaranteed instant notoriety.

Politicians of all stripes were fair game as far as The Eye-Opener was concerned. And in no uncertain terms. One cigar-smoking, not-too-popular politician found himself described as "a perambulating distillery with a smokestack attachment."

Edwards got sued a few times, but never successfully. At least one large rancher offered to punch him in the nose. But he wouldn't back down and wound up earning the grudging respect of even his victims. The much-maligned R. B. Bennett became a friend, and Edwards supported him in his election campaigns.

The one libel suit that amounted to something involved Robert Chambers Edwards as plaintiff and not, as might have been expected, the defendant. He sued one Daniel McGillicuddy, editor of a short-lived Liberal party organ, The Calgary News.

In a News article signed Nemesis, McGillicuddy accused Edwards of blackmail, slander and

81

smut, adding for good measure that the editor of The Eye-Opener "was born in a brothel and bred on a dunghill." Paddy Nolan and Bob Edwards took the issue to court. McGillicuddy was rapped verbally and fined $100. The next issue of The Eye-Opener reported:

"Poor old McGillicuddy has been a pretty sick man since his sentence. His physician pronounces it hog cholera. We hope to see him around town soon shaking hands with his many creditors."

McGillicuddy might have been expected to use that to sue Edwards. He left town instead. Fighting Edwards, as others had learned before him, was a lost cause.

Commenting on the pre-war real estate boom, The Eye-Opener noted that "everybody has a lot in mind. He wants to sell it or he wants to buy it." Anyone foolish enough to go broke buying and selling land got little sympathy. But an out-and-out swindle was something else.

A waitress in a favorite hotel told Bob she had been swindled and lost all her savings. The Eye-Opener ran the story, withholding the name of the crook but promising it would appear prominently in the next issue unless amends were made. The name never appeared. It was assumed amends were made.

As the real estate scramble reached ridiculous proportions, The Eye-Opener ran this alleged advertisement:

"Wanted by Calgary Real Estate Firm: Explorers to conduct parties out to their parks and additions. Must have natural topographical instincts. Indian trackers preferred. Good opening for Arabs used to the desert. Camels provided that can go for a month without water."

Bob Edwards' most unlikely campaign was on the side of the Drys when prohibition came up for a vote in 1915.

A story is told that the Wets offered Edwards a bribe, thereby assuring that the independent-minded editor would line up with the Drys. Actually, despite his own drinking habits, Edwards, as always, probably was just following the dictates of his conscience. He could see the ravages of unrestrained boozing all around him. He knew it at first hand. In 1915, prohibition offered a way out of a bad situation.

Edwards had a knack for picking winners and sometimes helped make winners out of them. He identified R. B. Bennett as a rising Tory star, supported the cause of women's suffrage and backed Henry Wise Wood, the agrarian leader who became the guiding genius of the United Farmers of Alberta.

He married late in life and, in 1921, the year that saw the UFA sweep into power in Alberta, he was elected to the Legislature as an independent.

He missed the celebration when prohibition carried the day in 1915, because he was in hospital sweating out another hangover, but he went on the wagon seriously when he ran for the Legislature. He delivered only one campaign speech (in favor of beer, as opposed to liquor) and in the Legislature he spoke only once (in favor of beer).

He died Nov. 14, 1922, and The Eye-Opener died with him.

In his *Eye-Opener Bob*, Grant MacEwan proposes that "average people" never reached the frontier. Those who first came and settled here were adventurers, different from the common run of people. They tended to think for themselves, they were independent, and more often than not they were at least moderate eccentrics.

Bob Edwards was a man for those times.

A
lively
society

It takes all kinds to build a community, and this community certainly attracted all kinds, including some odd species that seem practically indigenous to the foothills. In retrospect the frontier seems like an egalitarian sort of place, with everybody pulling together. But wealth, rank and privilege counted in the old days, just as they do now.

Bob Edwards clearly found more than enough pomposity and pretence all around him. By pointing at the sillier manifestations of class pride and laughing at them, The Eye-Opener may have helped to mitigate the social stratifications that naturally emerged in a new, growing city. Though the "better people" might scoff at The Eye-Opener, they knew that ostentation invited ridicule.

The working man, traditionally the backbone of any community, had pride in his craft. The stone masons, so numerous in the early days, knew they were helping to build something designed to last into the foreseeable future. There inevitably would be times of labor unrest, some of it serious, as workers sought due recognition and a seat above the salt at the bargaining table.

The condition of women in the early era would scarcely be tolerated today, though there were a few oddball exceptions. "Mother" Fulham, who kept pigs, was in her inimitably unwashed way as celebrated a character as anybody else in town.

At the other end of the social scale, Calgary generally always has been fascinated with royalty. At various times the whole town turned out to welcome Prince Erik of Denmark, Crown Prince Olav of Norway, and the Duc de Bourbon Palma of Luxembourg. The town was a long way from the glittering courts of Europe, and such visitors were a big deal.

The nurses of the Calgary General Hospital in 1912. Part of a burgeoning society, but one dominated by men.

Sketch made by Marquis of Lorne from 'the heights above Calgary'.

Not until May 26, 1939, when King George VI and Queen Elizabeth spent two hours here, did a reigning British monarch venture into these parts. Since then, royal visits have become almost common. Before then, the family at least was well represented by relatives and in-laws.

The Marquis of Lorne, governor-general of Canada, came here in 1881, two years before the railroad. His wife was Princess Louise, daughter of Queen Victoria, and nobody could get much higher up the social ladder than that. Louise was a natural when the time came to name that great lake up in the mountains.

The governor-general's unprecedented three-month tour was highly significant for Calgary's future. Among those who accompanied him were Sydney Prior Hall, artist for The London Graphic, reporters for The London Times and Telegraph and

The Toronto Globe, and Rev. Dr. James MacGregor, a Scottish clergyman who wrote voluminous accounts, all favorable, for The Edinburgh Courant and Scotsman.

This group, which included 77 persons in all, travelled by rail (as far as it went), steamboat, canoe and carriage until, in September, 1881, they reached "the heights above Calgary." Lord Lorne paused to sketch the scene. The sketch has survived, though the exact spot where he stood is hard to determine today.

A camp comprising 22 tents and 26 carriages was pitched "on a level and grassy plain, close by the banks of the Elbow." During the next three days the vice-regal party visited Rev. McDougall's mission at Morley, the Cochrane Ranch and John Glenn's farm. The group left Calgary Sept. 15, crossed the international border near Waterton,

The Marquis of Lorne, circa 1879.

and returned east by train through the northern U.S.

Somewhere along the way Lord Lorne was so captivated by the scene before him that he took time out to write a hymn, Unto The Hills. The exact site where he wrote it can't be verified, but it may be the vantage point, looking west from the Banff Coach Road, occupied today by the home of Frank Swanson, publisher of The Herald. In any case, the hymn is still in the hymn books of several denominations, and it remains highly popular.

The importance of the governor-general's trip was the effect it had on people back in Britain. Dr. MacGregor's articles induced many Scots to emigrate to the West, unfortunately often bringing their bagpipes with them. Sydney Hall's frontier art became famous, and upper-class Englishmen began arriving here to go homesteading.

Many tried to plant their old values in the new soil. Their first home might be a tent — with a piano in it. Two or three such instances have in fact been recorded. Wherever they came from, Calgary did acquire an upper crust. A few of the homes built here were comparable to those built by the grain barons of Winnipeg, which was settled much earlier.

Lower Mount Royal originally was developed by American land speculators who came here via the CPR. Some of the big cattle ranches found it more profitable to concentrate on breeding horses for shipment overseas as remounts for the British Cavalry. In many such ways, the frontier image grew dimmer.

In September, 1919, a mob of 40,000 royalists turned out to welcome the Prince of Wales. With cattle man George Lane's help, Edward acquired the E.P. Ranch in the Pekisko Hills, west of High River, and subsequently he came back every chance he got. He tried hard to mix into the ranchers' way of life. Rumor had it that some wild dice games took place at the E.P. Ranch.

The royal visitors were, however, transients. They helped spread the good word, but those who came to stay, not just to visit, had the task of directly shaping the city's character.

Dave Johnson, 92 years old and still active as custodian of the Al Azhar Temple on 17th Ave. until 1973, came to Calgary in a colonist car in 1905. He knew the old town well. He had at least a nodding acquaintance with most citizens, famous or otherwise. Not everyone patronized the Hull Opera House, but everybody pretty much knew everybody else in 1905.

Dave remembered the Alberta Hotel as "a gathering place for all the remittance men and their horses. The hitching post was out front. You dropped a rein and the horse stayed there."

Dave never stayed at the Alberta. That was for "society people," and he was a railway man. Railway and other workers lived mostly in boarding houses. They weren't grand, but they were the first home most single men had when they first came out here.

A typical boarding house charged tenants $10 a month. Men slept four to a room, or more if they could be squeezed in, and two to a bed. But there were compensations. Most houses were noted for "good substantial meals." Hot, substantial food was passed around big, substantial tables in large

bowls, first come, first served, and those who ate best were those with the longest and fastest boarding-house reach.

There was an immigration hall for newcomers, but guests could stay there only three nights. Then they had to make way for someone else. Newcomers in 1905 were pouring into town aboard every train.

Mr. Johnson recalled that the railroad had its own distinctive pecking order. The wiper worked in the shops, did the cooking, wiped down and cooled the engine, cleaned the ash can, and did everything else that nobody else wanted to do. On the road the fireman shovelled coal. The engineer sat majestically in his cab "and you did everything for him."

The aristocrats among the trains themselves were the silk trains. Running raw silk from the Orient to mills in New England, they had the right of way over everything else on the line. The CPR and CNR competed for the trade. It was an all-out race to see who could move it fastest — the raw silk couldn't be allowed to dry out — and the winners in the end were the U.S. lines to the south.

At least once a year, Dave Johnson would forego the boarding-house fare, don his best suit, and head for the dining room in the Alberta Hotel. At Christmas the menu offered "everything mentionable, all the wild life of the province, and of course always the big roast of beef."

Dave was earning nine cents an hour. Christmas dinner at the Alberta cost 75 cents. But it was worth the price. When you had paid your tab and were walking out, the management shoved a cigar box in front of you. Help yourself. They were very good cigars.

A man could be reasonably content in these circumstances, but only a few were anywhere near getting rich. To improve the working man's lot, the first labor unions began to emerge. At first they were guilds — engineers, firemen, brakemen, carpenters, machinists, and other specific trades — mostly associated with the railroad.

The Calgary Trades and Labor Council was organized in 1901. Original members included the railway guilds plus sheet metal workers, retail clerks and leather workers. In 1902 they added harness makers, draymen, printers and tailors.

There was a smidgen of labor unrest in 1902. Some carpenters and joiners struck. They wanted

The Wigwam, Calgary

Boarding house, named 'the Wigwam', was located at 334 - 12th Ave. S.W.

Edward visits the Calgary Golf and Country Club in Sept., 1919.

Prince of Wales with Alberta MLA, George Hoadley, right, and William Carlyle, ranch manager, inspect the E.P. Ranch in 1920's.

Getting ready for the 'Dominion Exhibition' in 1908.

Summer holidays were only days away when this Calgary class posed in 1919.

Bricklayers and Masons Union, after the Labor Day parade in 1906.

$2.50 a day for a nine-hour day. Some stone-cutters stopped work in a quarry, demanding 45 cents an hour for a nine-hour day and a shed where they could work during inclement weather. They got the shed.

The first Labor Day parade was held in 1902. Newspaper accounts record that 5,000 union members marched from Stephen Ave. to Victoria Park "wearing shining tin helmets and carrying white umbrellas." The significance of the white umbrellas wasn't explained.

By the end of 1902, labor was feeling its oats sufficiently to issue a "platform" demanding a minimum wage for all civic employees. The Calgary Labor Temple, incorporated May 30, 1912, erected the Labor Temple Building at 219 11th Ave. S.E.

The bleakest year in labor relations, immediately following the First World War, was 1919. Shock waves from the Winnipeg General Strike buffeted all of Western Canada. More than 25,000 union members walked out in Winnipeg on May 15, 1919. Support for the General Strike in Calgary was spotty and uneven, but 1,500 workers walked out in sympathy here on May 26.

The most fundamental issues were at stake — craft versus industrial unions, recognition of the union principle, wages, hours, and recognition of the "sympathetic" strike as a valid weapon.

The situation here never approached the situation in Winnipeg. There was trouble in the coal mines of southern Alberta and some unions struck, but others didn't. By June, 1919, the big news was that Germany finally had signed a peace treaty. By July, the city was preoccupied with the Calgary Exhibition. The next real union flare-ups wouldn't occur until the Depression.

In the stratification of classes, somewhere between the Prince of Wales and the One Big Union, the gang at the Alberta bar continued on its merry way. Bob Edwards, never wealthy but never a blue-collar man either, was the best known, but there certainly were others.

Among them was Paddy Nolan, who has been called "the greatest, wittiest criminal lawyer in Alberta, maybe in Canadian history."

The wit came naturally. Born in Limerick, Ireland, on St. Patrick's Day, 1864, he was the archetypal Irishman. By the time he settled in Calgary, he had been admitted to the bars of Ireland, England, and Canada's North West Territories.

"I've made it a point," Paddy proclaimed more than once, "to be admitted to every bar that would open its doors to me, and it was more than three, I assure you."

His credentials as a lawyer were confirmed in The Eye-Opener, which assured its readers that "all the best criminals go to Paddy Nolan."

He's celebrated as a defender of cattle rustlers and destitute widows. Actually his firm was one of the most prestigious in Calgary. At least once he acted for the government of Canada prosecuting rustlers. The fact about Paddy Nolan seems to be that he took cases that interested him. If the defendant happened to be a rustler or destitute widow, that was okay.

At 275 pounds, he was a formidable presence in court. And there's no doubt he was about the best after-dinner speaker in Calgary. In later years his son became a justice of the Supreme Court in Ottawa.

Among the other characters who helped enliven Calgary's early days, however briefly, was Max Aitken. R. B. Bennett was instrumental in bringing this fellow Maritimer to Calgary. Unlike Bennett, he didn't practise law. In 1898, the man who would become Lord Beaverbrook, kingpin of Fleet Street in London, England, was co-owner of a nine-pin bowling alley on 8th Ave.

His one-lane bowling alley was the city's first. Max and a partner would open the place at 6 p.m. For two hours one would set pins while the other took in the money. Then they switched for two hours. It didn't last long. A greater destiny awaited Max in England.

And then there was Mrs. John (Mother) Fulham, who demonstrated that if a future press lord could set pins in a bowling alley, a woman who kept pigs could face down the president of the CPR. In ways like this, the social distinctions tended sometimes to break down.

Mother Fulham kept pigs and a cow in a stable on 6th Ave. W. near the old court house site. She was known, however indelicately, as "the pig woman." To feed her pigs she collected swill from the rear of the hotels.

Legend has it that she took on the CPR after a locomotive killed her cow, and she took the dispute right into the railway president's car during a stop-over in Calgary. He promised to replace the cow. But Mother Fulham wept, since it was impossible to replace so fine a cow. Somehow, they got it straightened out.

Mother Fulham never made it into the society columns, except in The Eye-Opener. Mr. Fulham's exploits, if any, went unrecorded.

A lazy summer day in 1922: boating at Bowness Park. The park bandstand is in the background.

The innovators

Pat Burns, Eugene Coste and Peter Prince.

Pat Burns, Peter Prince and Eugene Coste didn't have much in common except that each provided the community with an essential service and became rich and famous. Others rushed off to the Klondike in 1898 looking for gold. Burns, Prince and Coste found better ways to make a fortune and leave a lasting impression.

Pat Burns gave the ranchers the means to get their cattle off the range and onto the dinner table. Peter Prince lit up the town with electricity. Eugene Coste gave the town natural gas — and scared the wits out of everybody in the process. His gas arrived with a hellish burst that looked capable of blowing the town away.

Pat Burns demonstrated as well as anybody how it was possible to come out here, make a lot of money, and stamp your name and your style on your city. Despite a lot of competition, it was Pat Burns who emerged as "Alberta's Cattle King." He was this country's answer to the giant meat packers who made Chicago a brawling, sprawling town.

It's said that he became a millionaire without ever losing a friend. Perhaps in his day that was possible, though it still sounds improbable. He's

been called, in a tolerant sort of way, an old cattle rustler. Actually he just had this single-minded talent for picking up every cow he could beg, borrow, or buy.

The result today is Burns Foods Limited. It's no longer the only packing plant in town. But, with a payroll of more than 4,000, it's the largest single employer in Alberta. In terms of annual sales, it's one of the top 15 corporations in Canada.

In stature Pat Burns resembled a stove in a colonist car. In his days of affluence, he was comfortably corpulent. Being in the food business, it was good advertising. But pictures of him portray a friendly, kindly soul, and that (no serious exceptions are recorded) is how he is remembered.

There are all kinds of legends about him. It's said he made his first million before he could sign his name. It's said he hung around the Alberta bar because he needed Paddy Nolan and Bob Edwards to help him with his arithmetic.

Though he indeed never got much by way of a formal education, his arithmetic reached formidable proportions before he was finished. At its peak his rangeland empire embraced 600,000 acres of land either leased or owned outright, 38,000 cattle, 1,500 horses and 20,000 sheep.

Born into an Ontario-Irish family of 11 in 1856, he came west with a brother in 1878. They acquired a homestead near Minnedosa, 140 miles west of Winnipeg, but Pat never was much of a farmer. He used his team of oxen and a wagon to haul hay to Brandon and freight from Winnipeg.

By 1885 he was supplying fresh meat to construction workers along the new railway line from Regina to Prince Albert. His chief asset was goodwill. He would get his steers from neighboring settlers, promise to pay for them in a month, deliver the beef, and rush back to settle his accounts.

He moved to Calgary in 1890 and sold beef to railway construction workers on the Calgary-Edmonton line. His first office was a shack on 9th Ave. opposite the site where the Palliser Hotel would be built more than 20 years later.

His packing plant here, the first in Western Canada, initially seemed to lack staying power. It burned down in 1892, and he rebuilt it. It burned down again in 1913. He was arranging to rebuild it, offering contracts on the the spot, before they had the fire out.

He cashed in on the gold rush in 1898 by shipping cattle north from Vancouver, driving them inland, slaughtering them, and floating the carcasses down the river to Dawson City. In Calgary in 1898, he was processing 150 cows weekly. By 1912 he owned six big ranches — one each near Fish Creek, on the Red Deer, Milk and Highwood Rivers, and two near Olds.

Acquiring more than 100 wholesale and retail outlets across the West, adding such grocery items

The Prince of Wales, centre, meets the Big Four: From left, Pat Burns, George Lane, A. J. McLean, A. E. Cross. The occasion was a visit by Edward to the E. P. Ranch around 1924.

Pat Burns: 1856-1937.

as creamery cheese and wholesale fruit, and opening overseas offices in London, Liverpool and Yokohama, Japan, he created one of the largest packing and provisioning businesses in the world.

Persistently he comes through sounding like the kind of tycoon anyone could like. His big pretentious house, on the present site of the Col. Belcher Hospital, was just one of many, including the Lougheed and Hull mansions, in that area. And, in many and various ways, he was a philanthropist.

The latch-string, it's said, always was out at all the Burns ranches. The latch-string was symbolic of the times. It was a piece of string, hooked to a lock and passed through a hole in the door so that anyone outside could pull it, lift the latch, walk in, and make himself at home.

One year, when district ranchers were enduring hard times, a Burns cattle buyer proudly reported to the boss that he had bought up a lot of cattle at a cent a pound less than the going price. Burns told him to go back and pay everybody the full price.

Sometimes he arranged to have the Catholic church in Midnapore painted. One year, when the job was done, everyone noticed how shabby the Protestant church looked. Burns promptly arranged to have the Protestant church painted, too. It wasn't a big thing, but at the time there were more bigots around than ecumenists.

Rows of Russian poplars lining No. 2 Highway south of Midnapore were planted by Burns when he owned the land. The three-mile stretch was dedicated as "Burns Trail" in 1943. Rocks for the Senator Pat Burns Memorial Gardens, on the North Hill below SAIT, came originally from the Burns mansion when it was torn down to make room for the Belcher hospital.

A grand birthday party was held at the Palliser Hotel July 6, 1931. More than 750 friends and admirers attended. Burns, 75 years old, remarked that it seemed a bit much for "an old cattle man." An announcement that he had been appointed to the Canadian Senate brought down the house.

Pat Burns was one of the Big Four who backed the first Calgary Stampede. The birthday party coincided with the opening of the 1931 Stampede. All the guests at the Palliser repaired to Victoria Park, where they unveiled a birthday cake that weighed three tons and stood 7½ feet high. They cut it up and distributed it among everybody attending the evening show.

Senator Burns didn't devote much time to the Senate. He died in 1937.

Peter Prince was a lumber man who, in the 1880s, said, "Let there be light." He hardly envisioned anything like the 10-storey Calgary Power Building at 110 12th Ave. S.E. An automatic timer turns on a system of vapor lamps that flood the building with light at dusk every night. The message is clear: Electricity is good for you.

When the first electric bulbs flickered alight here, away back when, not everyone was sure electricity was good for him. To ease the qualms of the faint of heart, a local hotel posted this sign in 1892:

"This room is equipped with Edison Electric Light. Do not attempt to light with match. Simply turn key on wall by the door. The use of electricity for lighting is in no way harmful

Interior view of Pat Burns & Company butcher shop in the early 1900s.

Ready and waiting for customers: The Burns shop around 1910.

to health, nor does it affect the soundness of sleep."

Today the City of Calgary is Calgary Power's biggest customer. In the beginning, though, there were no lights, and nobody seemed anxious to experiment with them. Then there was a great flap over who would supply the power. While the debate continued, everybody stumbled around at night in a perpetual blackout.

All the city had for illumination were oil and kerosene lamps and wax candles. They didn't make much of an impression. Accidents from people walking into one another in the dark were commonplace.

One who was stumbling around, and not enjoying it, was Peter Prince, Calgary general manager for the Eau Claire Lumber Company, of Eau Claire, Wisc.

The U.S.-based company had a big timber lease up the Bow River and a mill on the south bank of the Bow in Calgary. Both the general manager and the company were to lend their names to a part of the town. Prince's Island was named after Peter Prince, not the Prince of Wales.

The district between downtown and the Bow still is known as Eau Claire. If all goes well, part of the area will become the site of an integrated $180 million residential and commercial development called Eau Claire Estates.

Prince and the original Eau Claire company are long gone, but they never will be forgotten. In an article commemorating Calgary Power's 50th anniversary in 1961, Grant MacEwan provided this illuminating account of how Peter Prince became a power broker:

"It all began one dark night in early Calgary when, according to story, the sober and business-like Peter Anthony Prince of Eau Claire Lumber Company fell off a plank sidewalk and severely injured his well-groomed pride. While breathing anger at the unlighted streets, he vowed to make his adopted home the fifth community in Canada to have electric lights."

Before this, Prince had other things on his mind. The Eau Claire Company dredged a channel on the south side of the Bow so logs could be

Peter Prince: 1836-1925.

The Calgary Power dam over the Bow in 1911.

floated down to a mill at 2nd St. W. From 1887 the Eau Claire log drive was an annual spring event. Logs still were being driven down the river as late as 1944.

The company built the first traffic bridge over the Bow, near the present 10th St. bridge. River water kept the mill operating fitfully. Sometimes there wasn't enough water for the boilers. Other times there would be floods that would drive everyone away from the river.

Prince petitioned the town council in 1889 for permission to provide street lights. After a lot of bickering and haggling, poles were planted, wire was strung, and the first lights flickered on. Dimly.

There were a grand total of 300 lamps operating on partial power. Sourly observing the dull glow, citizens of the town figured they were better off with their candles. But they got the system up to full power before long, and the complaints subsided. Prince was happy. He finally could see where he was at, and he built himself a fine home on 4th Ave. not far from the mill.

Prince's original company was designated as the Calgary Water Power Company. Calgary Power didn't get into the act until 1911, and confusion between the two names persisted until Calgary Power Limited absorbed Prince's operation in 1928.

Calgary Power Limited was conceived and organized in Montreal. Directors closely associated with Calgary included R. B. Bennett, A. E. Cross and Max Aitken, who no longer was setting pins in a nine-pin bowling alley.

That Prince's original experiment worked says a lot for his staying power. Often the flow of the river would be slow or winter ice would almost stop it. As lights dimmed, the company turned to its mill for a reserve supply of power, stoking the steam engines with sawdust. The company sold its own bulbs, deliveries were uncertain, and often there were no bulbs to be had.

Calgary Power changed all that with huge hydro-electric plants all up and down the mountains and rivers to the west. When the Horse Shoe Falls dam was plugged into the City of Calgary electric system May 21, 1911, The Herald duly noted the significance of the occasion:

"The turning on of Calgary's hydro electric power was an event of immense importance to the city. It marked the beginning of a new era in its industrial development. Today, Calgary is released from coal-made power. She has stepped into the ranks of those fortunate cities to which the streams and waterfalls pay tribute."

In other words, the city now had light bulbs that more or less worked most of the time. Calgary Power completed what Peter Prince began, and the supply of electricity doesn't depend any more on the level of the Bow River as it ebbs and flows past Prince's Island.

Top photo: the Burns home at 4th St. and 12th and 13th
Avenues. Bottom photo: the 28-room Eugene Coste home
in Mount Royal, built in 1913.

Eugene Coste: he found gas.

If Peter Prince was the father of hydro-electric power in these parts, Eugene Coste played the same paternal role for natural gas. He is credited with bringing in the first commercial discoveries in both Ontario and Alberta, the former in 1889 and the latter in 1909. He definitely had a nose for gas.

The CPR, which still owned land all over the place, figured there might be oil or gas under some of it, and Coste was sent west in 1908 to see what he could find. He found gas. His discovery well, Old Glory, was located near Bow Island in the arid southeastern corner of Alberta near the South Saskatchewan River. Old Glory blew in on a cold February day in 1909.

Six more wells were drilled. They were all successful. By 1911, Coste computed that he had enough gas to supply Lethbridge and Calgary. He leased the rights to the new field from the CPR, organized his own company, and went to England looking for financing.

He called his company Prairie Natural Gas Company, and that was a mistake. No one in England ever had seen a prairie or smelled natural gas. They didn't know what Coste was talking about.

His solution was ingeniously simple. He changed the name of the company to Canadian Western Natural Gas, Light, Heat and Power Company Limited. Now he had no trouble raising money. Prospective backers might still think of gas mainly as an after-dinner phenomenon, but light, heat and power rang a bell.

A 16-inch pipeline, started April 22, 1912, was completed in just 86 days. Reaching 170 miles from Bow Island to Calgary, it was the third longest pipeline in North America.

Gas reached Calgary at a time when everybody was shovelling coal or burning wood. It was quite an event. An estimated 12,000 spectators assembled on Scotsman's Hill on the night of July 17, 1912, to see the inaugural flare turned on at 9th Ave. E. near the CPR tracks. They got more of a show than anyone bargained for.

Eugene Coste was master of ceremonies, assisted by his wife. At a signal from Coste, engineer Whitey Foster turned on the valve. To everybody's surprise, debris began to shoot up into the night sky — dust, stones and rocks, pieces of wood, then two or three pairs of overalls.

Then, while overalls wafted in the breeze, the gas burst through with a great roar. Uneasily, the onlookers backed away. Mrs. Coste stood her ground, shooting Roman candles at the standpipe, trying to light the flare. She succeeded, and with another great roar the flare illuminated the whole city.

Coste signalled his engineer to turn down the flow. Misinterpreting the order, the man at the valve opened it wider. A near panic ensued, with everybody backing off, yelling, and falling down. They finally got the flare — and the crowd — under control, and a full-scale stampede was averted.

In this manner was natural gas introduced to Calgary. Sources of supply other than Bow Island have been added since 1912, but never again with the same flamboyance.

Eugene Coste built himself a splendid home in Mount Royal, near 8th St. and 24th Ave. S.W., in 1913. From 1946 until 1959, Coste House was the home of the Calgary Allied Arts Centre. It was proposed in 1959 that the mansion become the "official residence" for Calgary's mayor. The idea never got off the ground, and the home was sold as a private residence.

Gallery

Andy Davison was mayor of Calgary for a record-breaking 16 years. He came to Calgary in 1918 and in 1921 was elected an alderman. In 1929 he was elected mayor by acclamation on his first try. Before retiring in 1945, he managed to work in eight years in the Alberta Legislature. During that time he refused to accept his mayor's salary. He died in 1963.

"A-A-A-A-H-H .... civilization".

In the summer of 1972 a series of street barricades were erected on streets leading into wealthy Mount Royal. The Mount Royal residents asked for the barricades to stop rush hour traffic from shortcutting through their neighborhoods on the way to and from work. The action sparked a conflict between the Mount Royal residents, who wanted protection for their community, and the commuting Calgarian, who wondered why Mount Royal should get such special treatment. Motorists were so upset with the privileged Mount Royal residents they resorted to occasionally ripping down the barricades, or leading parades of horn-honking motorists through Mount Royal streets in protest of the city's action. Eventually, all but one of the barricades were replaced by street signs prohibiting turns during rush hours, and a truce was declared.

The tornado struck at supper hour on June 25, 1915 and the storm that came with it caused floods that washed away railway lines and the wooden Centre Street bridge.

On Nov. 12, 1971, Air Canada Flight 812 left Calgary, bound for Toronto. Shortly after takeoff, Paul Joseph Cini, one of 118 passengers aboard, brandished a shotgun and demanded $1.5 million in ransom money. The DC-8 was diverted to Great Falls, Montana where $50,000 was picked up. The hijacked jet took off again only to return minutes later to allow the passengers to leave the plane. Once more it took off and this time Cini demanded to return to Calgary where, just before landing, Captain Vern Ehman subdued the hijacker. Captain Ehman then brought the jet down to a safe landing at the Calgary International Airport (photo) and five months later, Cini was sentenced to life imprisonment.

The world championship ski jumping competition was planned for the 1922 winter carnival in Calgary. Since the city couldn't supply a mountain, they built a ski jump on the Stampede grandstand roof. It was a good idea, though undoubtedly no one considered the possibility of a Chinook. When a Chinook did blow in, the inventive Calgarians simply went to Banff and imported the snow. And the show, photos left, went on.

Marlene Hashman, the daughter of millionaire developer, Sam Hashman, was abducted from her Bel Aire home in August of 1972 and held for 14 hours until her father paid a half million in ransom. Police recovered the money and found the kidnappers. Marlene, 17 at the time, was unharmed.

An animal island

The Calgary Zoo on St. George's Island, the biggest in Canada today and one of the best anywhere, began in a modest way.

No one was sure in the early days what should be done with the 42-acre island. At various times it was proposed as a site for a PoW camp, dog pound, isolation hospital, exhibition grounds, or a beer garden.

In 1922, a black-tailed deer from a travelling circus was presented to the Calgary Street Railway System, which had no place to keep the animal. First given a home at Bowness park, it later was transferred to St. George's Island.

The decision was made that the island should become a zoological park. Various citizens contributed a miscellaneous collection of pigeons, hawks and owls. A citizen with a bear cub in his back yard was told to get rid of it. He gave it to the zoo. Others chipped in with a goat, a swan and a kangaroo.

The Calgary Zoological Society was organized Oct. 28, 1928, with Dr. O. H. Patrick as president and R. B. Bennett, Pat Burns and A. E. Cross as patrons.

A severe setback occurred in 1929 when the Bow River flooded and washed away the bear and the goat. The city took over maintenance of the park, the society built pens and paddocks for the animals, and dikes were installed to control the flooding.

More than 1,000 trees and shrubs were planted in 1936. The Banff Zoo was abandoned the

First polar bear arrives in 1933.

following year, and much of its population moved to Calgary.

An English immigrant, Tom Baines, was hired as curator in 1929. During the next 40 years he built the zoo into what it is today. He literally worked 24 hours a day. His bachelor home was on St. George's Island, and he was available day and night.

The Dinosaur Park was started during the 1930s. Working with steel and mortar, Finnish-born John Kanerva recreated some 30 monsters from the dinosaur era. The most celebrated is "Dinny," a 65-ton Brontosaurus 90 feet long and 34 feet high.

Today the zoo has more than 1,400 live exhibits and attracts more than a million visitors annually.

Two sunny, noisy days in July

It was billed as "Festival Express" and for two sunny days in July of 1970, thousands of teenagers grooved to some of the best rock music Calgary has heard. Janis Joplin was "obviously the queen", as one critic noted, but the city police were also obviously at their finest as they kept order for the 23 hours the show ran. Hundreds of teenagers couldn't afford the $14 admission fee and had to dance to the rock music outside of McMahon Stadium.

The bus drivers went on strike in the summer of 1961 and Calgary motorists were quick to respond to the pedestrians' plight. The city erected directional signs at 16 downtown car-lift zones and soon car drivers were leaning out their windows to ask: "where are you going?"

The good life

The Calgary police department published a report in 1920 containing advertisements that were as informative as the report itself in describing what the city was like then.

Competition among the hotels was stiff. Daily rates at the Victoria Hotel were $1 and up. The St. Regis Hotel boasted telephones in every room. The King Edward Hotel had a bus that met every train. The Grand Union Hotel offered hot and cold water in every room.

The Bank of Hamilton offered 3-per-cent interest on all savings accounts of $1 or more.

The Zenith Cafe was "all newly decorated and sanitary" — and employed "a white chef!" The King George Hotel Grill offered an orchestra both at lunch and during the evening. The Billingsgate Fish Market claimed, in large type: "Fish make brains, and brains make money. Eat more fish."

"Dandruff is Disgusting," warned Harrison's Drug Store. "Harrison's special hair tonic is an absolutely sure fire dandruff eradicator. We believe it is the only one on the market."

James Proctor offered "scientific horseshoeing." Specialties of the Twin Stables were country trips and sleighing parties.

In May of 1945 an RAF Mosquito bomber, known affectionately as F for Freddie, crashed while taking off at McCall Field. The fighter-bomber had made 211 flights over Germany before being sent on a victory bond promotion mission across the country. On its visit to Calgary, it dazzled local residents with low-flying manoeuvres. When it struck an observation tower at the airport and crashed, the two-man crew died.

Remember the milk wagon? In this 1930 photograph the Co-op Milk driver had a horse to help him on his rounds. The company later became Alpha Milk and the horse was traded in for a motorized van.

The Wales Hotel, a Calgary landmark for 43 years, took just eight seconds to crash into oblivion. Most Calgarians were still asleep on Sunday morning, March 17, 1974, when 200 pounds of dynamite were detonated and the 11-storey hotel bit the dust.

When an airliner crash-landed at McCall in August of 1963, it gouged a path in a grain field. Kent Stevenson, then a photographer for The Herald, won a national newspaper Award for spot news photography with this picture.

An RCAF Golden Hawks jet collided with a civilian plane two miles west of the Calgary airport in August of 1959. The two men in the civilian plane were killed as was the pilot of the RCAF Sabre jet which is shown here.

The Capitol Theatre opened its Eighth Avenue doors in 1921 offering "The Love Special" as its first attraction. The theatre closed in April of 1972. It was the first Calgary theatre with sound in 1928 and the first with Cinemascope in 1953. The Palace theatre in 1926 showed "Calgary's Own movie" which was actually shot around Brooks.

The machines came in and churned up the concrete on 8th Ave., left photo, and by Stampede week, 1970, the first downtown street mall was finished. Then the controversy started. The two-block mall was designed to allow for buses, right photo, but they got in the way and were soon thrown off, just like the cars. Finally, in the spring of 1974, the machines came back again to tear up the mall and take out the bus platforms and the corrugated roadway that was forever tripping the unwary pedestrian.

The Second World War was just around the corner when King George the VI and Queen Elizabeth toured Canada in the spring of 1939. The royal couple arrived in Calgary at 3 o'clock on May 26.

The Herald has always "gone home", but around 1920 the circulation department used a pony cart to deliver the word to Calgarians.

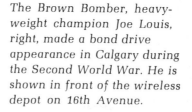

The Brown Bomber, heavy-weight champion Joe Louis, right, made a bond drive appearance in Calgary during the Second World War. He is shown in front of the wireless depot on 16th Avenue.

Former Mayor J. W. Grant MacEwan, left, reads the Speech from the Throne opening the Alberta Legislature 1966 session. It was his first session as the Queen's representative in Alberta and his appearance in striped trousers and topper, rather than the traditional Windsor uniform, created a mild surprise. The uniform didn't arrive in time for the February opening.

Wayne Harris, below, didn't play for the Stampeders in the 1973 season but he suited up just the same for a farewell ride around McMahon Stadium with his wife, Anne. Harris was a standout for a decade at the middle linebacker position before retiring at the end of the 1972 season.

Cowboy singer Wilf Carter got his first professional job singing with the CFCN Old Timers in the early 1930s. He was paid $5 per session.

Drinking gin for breakfast is a quaint Calgary custom associated with the annual Stampede.

Among the more hilarious Stampede traditions was the Sunday morning breakfast at Hays Farm in south Calgary. Senator Harry Hays held his first breakfast there with 800 guests in 1950. He estimates that about 68,000 invited guests attended the affair over the next 23 years.

Early-rising guests each year have imbibed large quantities of a mysterious drink called Sillabub. Senator Hays says, however, there isn't really much mystery about it. He believes it's originally an African drink. "It's mostly gin and fresh milk," the senator confides. The secret of mixing it is "not very much milk."

'Spitting a disgrace'

The headline on the front page of The Calgary Herald read: Neglect of City Police to Enforce Anti-Spitting Law Disgrace to Calgary. The date was Nov. 6, 1911, and the story read in part:

Why are Calgary police not enforcing the city by-law which makes spitting on the sidewalk punishable by fine? This is the question which many citizens are asking themselves at the present time.

A member of The Herald staff has been investigating this matter for the past few days, and as a result, it has been discovered that a disgraceful state of affairs prevails in certain sections of the city. The condition on the east side of Centre Street is simply disgusting.

Patrolmen stand idly by while men loaf on the edge of the sidewalk or lean up against the sides of buildings chewing tobacco, and every now and then expectorating right in the path of women who are forced to pass this way.

The university's rush to maturity

The University of Calgary in 1962.

The University of Calgary became an autonomous institution in 1966, but its history actually goes back to 1946, when a Calgary branch of the University of Alberta was established. The existing campus was opened in 1960 with two buildings — arts and education and science and engineering. The physical education building opened in 1962, and the library the following year. In 1964, Dr. H. S. Armstrong was appointed first president and the first degrees were awarded. In 1966 the university became autonomous from the U of A, and the Banff School of Fine Arts became part of it. In 1969, Dr. A. W. R. Carrothers became the university's second president. The 13-storey social sciences building was fully operating in 1970, and the first group of students moved into the married students' townhouse residence complex.

The U of C got its third president in 1974, when Dr. Carrothers left and Dr. W. A. Cochrane, former dean of medicine and provincial deputy minister of health, took over. The university's operating budget was $9.7 million in 1967 — it's $41 million in 1974. In 1966 the enrollment was 5,604 — but now full-time and part-time students number over 12,-000.

The land rush

Bustling downtown in 1912 reflected the boom-times era.

In 1912, when the city had a population of about 45,000, a committee of tub-thumpers began a campaign aimed at pushing the total to 100,000. Then the same group intended to reorganize and campaign again until the City of Business and Bustle by The Bow reached 200,000. The way it worked out, they would have had to wait 35 years to reach the 100,000 mark and 45 years to reach 200,000.

But there was no reason for anything other than wide-eyed optimism in 1912. The value of building permits that year was more than $20 million, a record that lasted until 1950. And $20 million bought a lot more in 1912 than in 1950. Or any year since.

The 1912 real-estate boom infected all of Western Canada. In Calgary, the new Hudson's Bay Company store and the Palliser Hotel were under construction. The new CPR station and the sandstone library in Central Park both were completed in 1912.

Big warehouses were being built all along 10th Ave. Substantial two-storey brick buildings were being built in the suburbs. Nearly all of them have survived. As often as not, the ground floor today is occupied by a friendly neighborhood corner store.

Extending only three miles east to west and one mile north to south in 1902, the city was bursting at the seams 10 years later. Everybody wanted a piece of the action. Nobody imagined that by 1913 most of the high rollers would be counting their losses.

Partly, perhaps, because of the packing plant, Calgary persisted in thinking of itself as another Chicago. The city was full of gee-whiz optimists dealing in properties guaranteed to make everybody wealthy.

For the fortunate few, there was a lot of money to be made. One of the more spectacular examples was a lot at 7th Ave. and 2nd St. S.W. It sold for $150 in 1895, $2,000 in 1905, and $300,000 in 1912. Its value today would be reckoned in the millions.

That particular lot happened to be in the middle of downtown. Other lots sold in 1912 aren't worth nearly as much now as they supposedly were worth away back then. Subdividers would take a quarter section, cut it up into 25-foot lots, and sell the lots for $1,000 to $1,200. Some of these sites are away out on the prairie, as far away as Chestermere Lake.

Somewhat closer in, "American Hill," where houses once reached only part way up the slope because horses couldn't climb any higher, came into its own as Mount Royal, where many years later they would try to erect barricades to keep the cars out.

American Hill, so named because so many U.S. land speculators accumulated there, was an early symbol of American imperialism. The CPR, while it still owned the land, tried to stem the invasion. When they changed the name to Mount Royal they also gave the streets "Canadian" names, including French-Canadian names such as Montcalm, Joliet, Frontenac, Cartier and Marquette that the foreigners up there presumably couldn't pronounce.

Ironically, the Americans reclaimed portions of Mount Royal during the post-Leduc oil boom. At least part of it became American Hill all over again.

Pending construction of Centre St. Bridge in 1915-16, the North Hill was slower to develop. The main push was south and east, where land was sold in districts that wouldn't have a house on them until long after Leduc. Beyond even that, the city annexed land in 1912 that was abandoned a few years later and still sells as acreage for farms or pasture.

The building boom, though real enough, precipitated a much more fanciful real-estate boom. Construction in the downtown sector reached the point where builders were complaining about a cement shortage. The real worth of the land being sold diminished in proportion to its distance from the city centre.

As Bob Edwards said, everybody had a lot in mind. Under the heading, Two Society Girls Who Have the Realty Fever Bivouac in Automobile, The Calgary Albertan reported in April, 1912, how "two young women of social prominence camped out all night in a big touring car on the curb," waiting to buy lots in the morning.

Would-be buyers often stood in line all night waiting to give away their money. If it rained, they were given a ticket designating their place in the queue. They had to return every hour to redeem it.

A lot on 1st. St. W. sold in February, 1910, for $16,450, and in January, 1912, for $75,000. A clerk in

Mount Royal homes in 1916 — an early symbol of American imperialism.

The Mawson plan: sketch shows how Calgary could have looked.

the land titles office who bought a lot in 1904 for $825 sold it to "a syndicate of British capitalists" in 1911 for $105,000. His profit: $104,175.

Another Big Day in Calgary Real Estate was almost a standing headline in all of the local newspapers.

At the first CPR land sale, a lot at 8th Ave. and Centre St. sold for $250. The Bank of Commerce occupied it in 1913. The estimated value of the land alone, a 1,000-per-cent increase, was $250,000.

Some of these prices, reflecting the temper of the times, were wildly inflated. The size of the lots sold in 1912 wasn't always specified, making comparisons difficult. Today, an average 25 by 130-foot lot in the downtown renewal area is worth about $40 to $50 a square foot. A few blocks farther west, it's $100 and up.

The new City Hall, costing $300,000, was opened in 1911. Still in use, it hasn't been a bad investment. In 1911, however, the cost forced the mill rate up to 14½ mills and taxpayers were not happy.

The City Hall originally was "set in a flowering

oasis of palm trees," according to press reports. To decorate the site they imported 210 palm trees, and one of them lasted until 1935. Early pictures of the sandstone building show a cannon near the main entrance. Its purpose isn't clear, unless it was to ward off attacks of irate ratepayers.

A newspaper advertisement in 1911 listed two lots in Happyland at $275 "with easy terms." Wherever Happyland was, the price was right.

Another advertisement listed a splendid well-built house in Mount Royal with a fine view, eight rooms, four bedrooms, steam heat, fireplace, and corner lot. The realtor estimated the place could be rented for $60 a month. The purchase price, $2,000 down, was $7,000.

In 1910, a full acre of undeveloped land in Mount Royal was offered for $4,700. But that kind of bargain didn't last long. The CPR placed caveats on the Mount Royal district prohibiting commercial developments and requiring that all new houses be worth at least $3,000.

The railway's interest in the district lasted for many years to come. A few CPR lots, presumed to

1912 — the city sets a dizzy pace

A crowded 8th Avenue in 1912 when land went for inflated prices.

The Stampede parade with the crowd watching the post office entry pass by.

The 1st St. West subway looking north with the Palliser Hotel going up behind it.

The Duke of Connaught initiates Calgary's street fire alarm system.

be the last, were sold there shortly after the Second World War.

Fred Charles Lowe, a realtor, is credited with opening up most of the south part of the early city, including Elbow Park, Elboya and Windsor Park. Lacking bulldozers in those days, landscrapers used streams of water to cut away parts of the bank of the Elbow River.

With all this activity, it's quaint to note that, in 1915, there still was a "ranche" at 17th Ave. and 14th St. S.W., and a duck slough near 22nd Ave. and 21st St. S.W. The Frontier Stable, on the northeast corner of 8th Ave. and 2nd St. S.W., survived until 1911.

With down payments pegged as low as $1, anybody who could scrape together a few dollars speculated in real estate during the 1911-1912 land rush. But the notion that everybody was going to get rich was, of course, a myth. By 1913 the money tree had dried up. Some overseas speculators discovered too late that they had been induced to buy, sight unseen, lots situated beneath the Bow River.

Thoughts about planning first occurred to the city in 1911. A planning commission was appointed, but its duties were somewhat limited. Its chief concerns were street lights, tree planting, cleaning up unsightly vacant lots, and improving the standard of garbage cans.

Something more substantial obviously was needed, and in 1913 the city hired Thomas Mawson, an English town planner with an international reputation reaching from Copenhagen and The Hague to Vancouver, B.C., where he designed Stanley Park.

In 1913 his timing was bad, but Mawson set to work planning for a city of 500,000. It would be the centre of a rich farming empire with a population of not less than 3 million.

To begin with, he wanted to know why the streets in a brand-new city hadn't been laid out much wider. The answer, that narrow streets meant less mud to wade through when crossing them, didn't satisfy him.

He didn't approve of the grid system of laying out streets. "Your gridiron system of planning," he admonished the city council, "leads to great loss of momentum owing to all fast wheeled traffic having to pull up every time it approaches the end of a block."

Instead, Mawson designed a city of skyscrapers based on a wagon-wheel pattern. Radial roads would break up the monotony of city blocks. From the planner's drawing boards sprang a concept for a new Paris of the Prairies. The drawings today may resemble Moscow more than Paris, but in many respects Mawson was away ahead of his time.

He recommended wider streets, more bridges, subways, rapid transit, and enclosed sidewalks and malls from 8th Ave. to Prince's Island. At a time when Nose Hill and Fish Creek were far removed from everything, he suggested "a beautiful belt of parks all around your city." Every home would be within reach of open park space.

Mawson's idea for a bridge at Centre St. wasn't so good. Noting that the north side rises much higher than the south side, he proposed a flat crossing with an elevator at the north end for trolley cars and other vehicles.

If they had gone ahead with that arrangement — and bids actually were accepted for hoisting equipment — today's traffic bottlenecks during rush hours north of the river would be plain ridiculous. Cars would be stacked up for miles back waiting for their turn on "the lift."

Other Mawson proposals, however, still turn up today under the heading of new business. Some of his ideas are as valid now as they would have been in 1913. The trouble then was that Calgary's first big boom had run its course. The party was over.

The real estate boom ended at about the time the first Turner Valley oil boom began. Then the oil rush, too, subsided due to the First World War. Everybody sort of assumed the good days would return after the war. They didn't.

The Hudson's Bay store and the Palliser Hotel opened in 1914. Then, for a long time to come, everything stopped. In 1917, not one new house was built in Calgary. It was 1928 before the number of building starts equalled the pre-war total for 1914.

The $1 million T. Eaton Company store was opened by Lady Eaton in 1928. The Hudson's Bay Company completed a major addition in 1929, and in 1929 "an all-round improvement in business conditions" was cited in the press. Then the roof fell in again.

Dry days, wet days

References to Calgary as "a great saloon town" keep turning up here and there throughout the town's early history. The impression is that of a wide-open town where everybody constantly staggered around in a state of advanced inebriation.

There was a time when the bars were about as wide open as they could get. But there also were times of out-and-out prohibition. And the "saloon" of frontier mythology didn't play a big role here. The so-called saloons were licensed bars connected to hotels. Even in the free and easy days, they had that veneer of respectability.

Booze unquestionably played a major role in the settlement of the West. The first American fur traders brought it into the country. The Mounties came west specifically to put an end to the whisky trade.

Before Calgary existed as a viable community, the council of the North West Territories passed an order-in-council authorizing anyone finding anyone else with liquor in his possession to make a citizen's arrest. The North West Territories Act of 1875 prohibited the importation, sale, or possession of liquor except when imported via a permit signed by the lieutenant-governor.

Enforcing this kind of prohibition produced headaches among drinkers and non-drinkers alike. If many of the early settlers were two-fisted drinkers, many more were teetotallers. They objected to whisky on religious grounds. Caught in the middle between the wets and the drys, the Mounties' enthusiasm for the liquor laws left everything to be desired.

Beer drinkers celebrated the 1933 Stampede at the York Hotel tavern.

The chief victims obviously were the Indians. In the very early days, one buffalo hide would buy two cups of unholy gunk. A typical concoction sold to the Indians consisted of a gallon of rum mixed with two pounds of chewing tobacco, red peppers or ginger. Add red ink or pain killer and water, and boil it. The recipe made five to 10 gallons of whatever you wanted to call it.

The Mounties managed to clamp down on the trade with the Indians, but some of the early policemen were a problem themselves. The editor of an early newspaper felt obliged to editorialize as follows:

"It is bad enough for a civilian to get drunk and whoop about the streets but it is much worse for a policeman. We trust we shall not be obliged to speak of a similar occurrence again. But really, this blazing away with a pistol whenever a man gets drunk, whether it is in the hands of a policeman or a citizen, is getting monotonous."

While the majority of the population might have subscribed to the liquor laws, those who didn't were ingenious in circumventing them. Getting a permit was troublesome, and most of the supply was smuggled in.

The police raided one of the first trains into Calgary and intercepted 40 gallons of whisky and two dozen bottles of brandy hidden in barrels of oatmeal. Whisky also arrived in barrels marked kerosene, varnish and barn paint. Hollow tin "bibles" were found to contain gin.

Intercepted shipments were supposed to be destroyed. First, however, the contents had to be identified. Volunteers for the task were readily available. By the time they were finished, there often would be nothing left to destroy.

Most of the Mounties were more than willing to participate in such investigations. A member of the original force recorded this item in his diary:

"We were not supposed to drink but we could always get whisky. Some men even took the horse's medicine and drank it. I don't know what was in it but if you drank enough you could sure get high."

Mounted Police historian Ronald Atkin puts the booze business into what sounds like an accurate perspective:

"Strong addiction to liquor among the members of a force whose main purpose was the strict enforcement of prohibition was a continuing problem (but) drinking was regarded by the men themselves as one of their few escapes from the tedium of life in an empty, undeveloped country."

The Mounties did their best to entertain themselves in a respectable fashion. They organized their own bands. But such diversions didn't keep a young, virile, and pretty wild lot satisfied indefinitely. If the booze was available they would go on an occasional "bust", then shake it off and get back to work.

The "dry" campaign received support from the Hillhurst Presbyterian Sunday School.

A reporter for The Toronto Globe who visited Calgary in 1888 wrote about encountering "vile whisky" called 40-rod, so named because it was "reputed to kill at that distance." Whatever it was, it was easy to get:

"One had only to mount a flight of stairs, give a mysterious knock, and be admitted to a luxurious bar and drink with the leading citizens of the town."

In 1892, bowing to the inevitable, the territorial authorities abandoned prohibition in favor of licensed hotels. New towns were springing up all over the landscape, and hotel rooms were urgently needed. Prospective hotel-keepers argued persuasively that they couldn't operate at a profit without a liquor licence.

Once they got their licensed bars, the hotel men in Calgary went into a huddle and came out with a uniform price list: straight whisky two drinks for a quarter, mixed drinks 25 cents, beer two for 25 cents, champagne $2.50 to $4.

For the first time the customers knew — or at least thought they knew — what they were getting for their money. A customer at the Alberta Hotel could be pretty sure he was getting what he was paying for. Elsewhere, the label on the bottle and the contents might be two different things.

The bars proliferated and prospered until 1915. They had a distinctive odor that was all-pervasive. It was part beer, part whisky, and something more. Calgary author James H. Gray, in a book called *Booze*, a history of booze, bars and prohibition on the Prairies, described the atmosphere:

"Bars were made more odoriferously offensive by an assortment of smells all their own. Livery stables were hard by the hotels. The aroma of the stables was wafted barward on the evening breezes that came behind the rain, mixed with trade smells that stuck to the clothing of the workers. Railway shop-workers smelled of cinders and machine oils, the slaughter-house had its own odors."

The Calgary Herald related that "Calgary is quartered into three halves: East Calgary, West Calgary and the Brewery. To some minds the greatest of these is the Brewery, but that is a matter of taste entirely."

115

The brewery came into being through an accident. A. E. Cross, one of the district's Big Four cattle ranchers, was injured while trying to ride what was described as "a difficult horse." His doctor advised him to seek a less strenuous occupation. Looking around, he decided Calgary needed a brewery.

He was not one for half measures. He studied and acquired diplomas at the Montreal Brewing Company, the U.S. Brewers' Academy of New York, and the Wahl-Henins Institute of Fermentology in Chicago. Then some over-eager Irish brewers almost spoiled it all by breaking open a keg of immature beer on St. Patrick's Day, several days before it was fit to drink.

The day of the "green" beer was only a temporary setback. Calgary Brewing and Malting's product, given time, proved eminently satisfactory, the townspeople lapped it up, and the company prospered.

Alfred E. Cross started a brewery and became one of the city's leading citizens.

In such benign circumstances, the Cross family became leading citizens. A. E. Cross was a founder of the Western Stock Growers' Association, the Calgary Board of Trade, the Ranchmen's Club, the Calgary Golf and Country Club — and the Stampede. The brewery-operated Horsemen's Hall of Fame still helps perpetuate the rangeland heritage.

By 1904, Calgary had a population of 9,554 and a three-man police force. Most of the hotels on 8th Ave. were situated on the south side of the street. The ladies, it's related, chose to walk on the north side. It sounds in retrospect like one big, long drunken party. But the fact is uncontrolled boozing was having its inevitable effect.

Pay-cheques as often as not tended to be cashed and spent the same day. "Treating" was a wide-spread custom causing a lot of trouble. It's an old story: if someone buys a round he's going to stay put until everybody else buys a round.

The whole business got sufficiently out of control by the time of the First World War that the city — the West, in fact — was ready for prohibition. Farm leaders such as Henry Wise Wood were dedicated supporters of prohibition. And they had plenty of support from city dwellers fed up with what they felt had become intolerable excesses.

A plebiscite was held in 1915. The night before the vote, thousands of prohibitionists ignored a sudden thunder storm and marched through the streets proclaiming their cause. In Alberta the vote for prohibition was 58,295 to 37,509. The Alberta Temperance Act came into effect July 1, 1916. The Alberta Hotel was converted into a retail and office block.

The popular view today is that prohibition was a failure. James Gray emphatically disagrees. He says:

"Every claim which the moral reformers made for prohibition turned out to be true. It did reduce alcoholic consumption, perhaps by as much as 80 per cent. It did immediately improve the economic status of the working class. It did very substantially improve industrial efficiency by reducing absenteeism. It did reduce drunkenness and rowdiness in the streets. It did result in a marked reduction in all other forms of crime."

The statistics are impressive. Between 1914

and 1918 the Calgary police department went from 63 constables who made 2,550 arrests for drunkenness and vagrancy to 28 constables who made 183 arrests for liquor offences.

The great prohibition experiment might after all have worked if it had been given a better chance. But there were gaping loopholes in the law all along.

Interprovincial trade in liquor was banned only briefly. A ridiculous situation existed where Calgary could get its supply from Moose Jaw and Moose Jaw could get its supply from Calgary. They were in separate provinces.

Druggists could prescribe alcohol, and it was remarkable how many citizens seemed to have chronic ailments requiring alcohol for proper treatment. The breweries, operating under federal charters, stayed in business. So-called Temperance beer (two per cent) still could be obtained in the hotels.

Rum-runners were busy across the prairies and across the border. They were blamed for a few bank robberies here and there, but Canada never produced anything resembling an Al Capone. There were no St. Valentine's Day massacres in these parts.

The bank robberies occurred in the smaller towns where there were no police. Skilled safe-crackers would slip into town at night, cut the phone and telegraph wires, and blow the safe. The townspeople might hear the noise, note that someone was robbing the bank, and go back to sleep hoping the thieves got away with the bank's notes and their debt records.

Prohibition lasted eight years, and perhaps it could have lasted longer if everybody had just stopped yelling and let it work itself out. Regardless of the law, the well-to-do maintained full cellars, the middle class had its prescription service, farmers had their stills, urban workers

"At least it will keep them off the streets!"
— Tom Innes cartoon notes the appearance of 18-year-olds in the Calgary bars.

could have had home-made beer and wine, and the majority that voted for prohibition could have carried on nicely with soda pop.

It was widely believed that women carried the day for prohibition while the men were away at war. But another plebiscite after the war verified the results of 1915. What finally killed it was inadequate enforcement, too much rigidity, and the idea that government liquor stores could become a very valuable new source of revenue for the provinces.

In 1924, Albertans returned to the polls and gave the government a mandate to sell all liquor and to regulate beer sales in licensed premises. Prohibition still collected 61,780 votes, province-wide. But 93,490 voted for the new deal and started arduously filling out order forms at liquor-store counters.

Until 1958 the licensed beer parlors were segregated. For a couple hitting the pubs for a gay,

mad night on the town, it was an absurd arrangement. The boy went in one door, the girl disappeared behind a different door, and that was it until they staggered out again, if ever. It didn't do anything for sociability.

Facilities were provided for "ladies and escorts" in 1958, and much more has changed since then. The choice today is wide-ranging, from taverns to well-stocked bars and dining lounges or cabarets, with or without live entertainment. Eighteen-year-olds joined the drinking crowds (legally) in 1971, when the age of majority was reduced from 21.

Booze always has been and undoubtedly always will be a highly debatable topic. In Calgary's case it seems that the days of the wide-open "saloons" were too much, prohibition might conceivably have worked, present facilities are all right if they aren't abused, and maybe something different like neighborhood pubs would be nice. Or maybe not. It's a matter of opinion.

Sirens

The paddy wagon joins the police force in 1920.

The old wide-open cowtown has evolved into a peaceable sort of city. You can book a bet in Calgary, pick up a girl and buy hard drugs, but the operators are mostly amateurs. If organized crime has made inroads into the city, it has succeeded in keeping a low profile.

There were 10 murders in Calgary in 1971, and the populace was duly alarmed. But Washington, D.C., counted 300 murders in 1971. Two years later, Detroit achieved additional notoriety with a grand total of 750.

A local police spokesman points out that "you could move our situation south of the border and any city there would be pretty happy with it."

The original policy of the North West Mounted Police perhaps is best summed up by a ringing declaration attributed to Ephraim A. Brisebois. He is reputed once to have silenced a recalcitrant whisky smuggler by telling him, flatly: "We make up the law as we go along."

In 1884, an unemployed laborer raided a dry goods store, killed a clerk with an axe, rushed out, and was nabbed in the street. He was tried, convicted, and hanged. This sordid affair is noteworthy only because it was the first murder — and first hanging — officially recorded here.

The town organized its own police force in 1884. The initial force consisted of three men. The chief constable was Jack Ingram. He was also the licence inspector, dog and cat catcher, and keeper of the pound.

For many years the local force unfortunately kept no records, either because the idea never occurred to anybody or there were some aspects of law enforcement that were best left unrecorded. The Historical Society of Alberta has attempted to fill the gap with a resume of "Calgary jails and the police force" culled from old newspaper files.

Prior to 1884 the Mounties were responsible for all law and order, and prisoners were detained in a little log shack near Centre St. in the lane between 7th and 8th Ave.

Legend has it that the first jail was built by two local lawyers, who on the day of its completion staged a celebration, got drunk, and were locked up. Since they had built the place, they had no trouble escaping from it.

A local character billed as the strongest man in town also demonstrated how the new jail was less than escape-proof. Locked up, he kicked his way through the slab roof and took off. He was recaptured along the Elbow River, roped, hog-tied, and hauled back.

During the Riel Rebellion of 1885, Col. Walker was appointed to organize and arm the settlers. He wound up with an army of occupation consisting of 106 leading citizens, all packing guns and sworn in as special constables. It was the biggest police force on duty in Calgary at one time for many years to come.

Tom English became chief constable in 1891 and remained at the helm until 1909. He was another of those legendary characters that the climate here seems to encourage. He managed to keep himself both prominent and controversial by running the department pretty much according to his own whims.

Chief English subscribed to Ephraim Brisebois' philosophy that the law is something you make up as circumstances dictate. Houses of ill repute thrived during his regime. After a final falling-out with the city council, he was fired in

Calgary police force at turn of century; Chief Tom English fifth from left.

1909. He wound up as an immigration agent at a time when new settlers were pouring into the district in record numbers.

In 1908, a combined city hall and police headquarters was built at 7th Ave. and 2nd St. S.E. It was an odd-looking structure. The council chamber and court room occupied main-floor quarters resembling a stable. The police occupied a two-storey section with a belfry.

Four police cells in the rear of the building were usually full, mainly because of fist-fights. Brawling was a community pastime. Police would break up a fight, incarcerate the combatants, then go out and break up another fight. It was a full-time job.

During the era of the stipendiary magistrates, the going rate was about $2.25 per case. The more cases they heard, the more these justices of the peace earned. If the police sometimes lacked incentive, the court never did. If there were no

In 1942 army officers trained these Calgary policemen to fire bren guns and Tommy guns. After a 2-month course, they were "ready for any emergency."

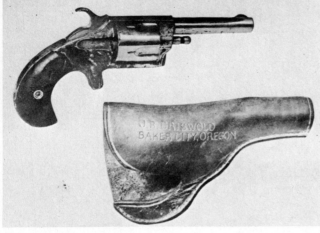

About 3.10 a.m. Tuesday, 13th June, 1933, Inspector Joseph Carruthers, City of Calgary Police Department, was shot and killed by some person at present unknown, and a reward of $1,500.00 has been offered for information leading to the arrest and conviction of the person responsible.

"Joe Carruthers murdered by unknown thief in city," read the headline the day after the Calgary police inspector was shot in a lane. Carruthers had been called to investigate reports of a prowler in June, 1933 when he was shot, precipitating "the most determined and intensive manhunt in Calgary police history". The revolver in the illustration was found in the river and police believed it was the murder weapon. In 1957 police closed the file, revealing a man in a mental institution was responsible.

cases on the docket, the magistrate couldn't earn his keep.

Thomas Mackie took over a 26-man force in 1909. The department had a police horse and democrat, but it wasn't fast enough to catch anything. A mounted section was added in 1910. Chief Alfred Cuddy acquired the first police automobile in 1912. David Ritchie, chief from 1919 to 1941, added radio-equipped cruiser cars.

Sam Patterson (1941-1950) hired the force's first-ever policewoman. He was succeeded as chief in turn by Malcolm Boyd, Reginald Clements, James McDonald, Larry Partridge, Ken McIver, M. J. "Duke" Kent and Brian Sawyer.

The city almost hired an American chief — Charles Gain, of Oakland, Calif. — after Duke Kent, but the appointment of an American proved too controversial. Amid charges of narrow nationalism, City Council voted 7-5 in 1972 in favor of a Canadian chief. While the debate still raged, with the rest of the country joining in, Gain quietly withdrew from the race.

When the new city hall was completed in 1911, the police department moved into the basement. Then a big brick building just east of the city hall was headquarters from 1914 until May 25, 1961, when the boys in blue abandoned the old "cop shop" and occupied their present modern headquarters at 316 7th Ave. S.E.

The nature of the policeman's duties has changed radically over the years. Gradually, through bylaws and orders from the chief's office, a nondescript and pretty independent lot acquired discipline and new responsibilities.

Traffic became a problem prior to the First World War. The city enforced a speed limit of six miles per hour for horses or horse-drawn vehicles, 10 miles per hour for cars except at intersections, where the limit was five miles per hour.

A 1912 bylaw prohibited motor-driven machines in moving picture theatres. Projectors had to be operated by hand. A 1913 bylaw prohibited kettle, pan and tea-tray bands, horn-blowing, bell-ringing, singing, shouting, and loitering. These bylaws have all long-since been repealed, although excessive noise-making is still frowned on.

Chief English, in 1902, was the first to set down a list of rules governing the conduct of the force. Members of the force were required to keep their hair cut so it looked smart and clean. Beards were allowed if they didn't conceal "the number or the letter on collar or coat."

Borrowing money from a saloon keeper was prohibited. Laughing or joking with prisoners was frowned upon. And "members of the force will, on discovering any pickpocket in any crowded place,

A mounted city police officer patrols during the 1912 Stampede. One of their duties was to chase away stray cattle.

Calgary police used the call box system as far back as 1914 when 67 were installed covering every part of the city.

The Nose Creek "Red Light" district on a Sunday afternoon in 1910.

call out in a loud voice and give notice of such characters being present."

Chief Cuddy issued another set of rules in 1912. They were designed to cope with any eventuality.

Acrobats performing in the streets were to be cautioned against causing danger, obstruction or annoyance. Open-air preachers could be left undisturbed unless they caused "an actual obstruction of a public thoroughfare." Police were to prevent boys from flying kites where danger or annoyance might be caused. Children trundling hoops through the streets were to be told to stop doing it or their hoops would be confiscated.

The police department published its own progress report in 1920, leading off with this glowing statement:

"Calgary is an ideal town to live in. Business, health and pleasure — all can be enjoyed in full measure by its happy and uniformly prosperous citizens."

The report's summary of police activities during the previous year suggests that not everybody was either happy or uniformly prosperous. A total of 3,737 cases were tried in police court in 1919. The breakdown describes an extraordinary variety of activities. Among the cases cited for 1919 were these:

Brand Act 3, buying unwholesome eggs 1, cheating at play 1, cattle stealing 2, drunk 475, desertion from army 4, exhibiting indecent pictures 1, frequenter of disorderly house 240, fortune telling 3, horse stealing 5, insanity 25, inmate of bawdy house 28 (female), keeping bawdy house 4 (male), 39 (female), keeping gaming house 12, keeping opium joint 2, Lord's Day Act 12, Loafer Law 18, motor vehicle act 547, Mischievous Animals Act 1, opium and drug act 88, preventing delivery of a telegram 2, seduction under promise of marriage 3.

Disorderly houses, bawdy houses, gaming houses, opium joints? Through the statistics filters a picture of a town that was naughty, not uniformly nice.

As early as 1905, cab drivers were warned sternly that anyone chauffeuring "any prostitute or woman of ill fame in uncovered vehicles" could have his licence revoked. Driving the girls around was all right, but not in uncovered vehicles.

The law provided that prostitutes couldn't be arrested just because they were prostitutes. Constables were to make careful note of activities surrounding all houses of ill-fame, but that was all. Only inspectors of divisions were authorized to take further action, if any.

During the boom of 1912, Calgary's bars, brothels and gambling houses evidently were celebrated far and wide. The painted ladies of the night took over first the area east of downtown, then the Hillhurst district north of the river, and later the Nose Creek valley.

Calgary's well-equipped firemen displayed their apparatus for the photographer around 1913-14.

The fire department's first steam engine with Captain James Smart in the foreground.

The red-light district along Nose Creek thrived during 1912 and 1913. Some houses had pianos, and hired piano players, and they could be heard half a mile away on Scotsman's Hill.

When the pre-war boom ended the houses gradually emptied, were torn down or burned down, and after the Second World War the Nose Creek coulee itself disappeared when the city converted it into a garbage dump.

In his book *Red Lights on The Prairies*, Jim Gray describes Pearl Miller's "25-year reign as Calgary's most famous prostitute". She was so popular that during the Second World War the Princess Pats allegedly erected a memorial to her. It read: *"To hell with Pearl Harbor, remember Pearl Miller."*

Mr. Gray concludes that the slogan was obviously a fabrication, yet "the story really ought to be true of a city where the most famous woman in its entire history was the keeper of a common bawdy-house."

Whether Pearl Miller indeed was the city's most famous woman is debatable. Others must have a more legitimate claim. Infamous is perhaps a more appropriate word to describe Pearl. Her "25-year reign," however, does seem to warrant a place in the archives.

The history of the fire department parallels that of the police department, but tends to focus on one redoubtable individual — Cappy Smart. When you remember the fire department, you have to remember Cappy Smart. He was the all-time, prototypical, smoke-eating fireman.

The need for a fire department was apparent as early as Jan. 5, 1885. The inadequacy of existing fire-fighting methods was amply illustrated in this report in The Calgary Herald:

"J. L. Bowen's $575 house on Atlantic Avenue West went up in smoke on Monday afternoon. Great credit is due to the able way in which Mr. Collingham saved the henhouse. Mr. C. noticed the trepidation of the hens, and guessing intuitively that the henhouse, which was five yards from the fire, was

Firemen battle blaze in Woolworth store at 106 - 8th Ave. S.W. in 1921.

getting hot, he encircled the structure with a rope and hauled it away to a place of safety."

A bucket brigade was present, but its water cart wasn't working. A crowd assembled, including the mayor and council. They threw snowballs at the fire. The Herald concluded that what the town needed was a fire engine.

Originally, all the firemen in town were volunteers. It was 1909 before the city acquired a full-time, 40-man fire department. Before that volunteers were paid 75 cents per call, an arrangement that assured 100 per cent attendance at every fire, large or small.

In 1904, the department consisted of 35 active volunteers and 20 reserves. Ten men slept at the fire hall, then situated adjacent to the present Canadian Legion Hall at 116 7th Ave. S.E., and the rest were connected by an alarm system. A city-wide alert would disrupt half the boarding houses in town.

As for the 75 cents per fire — plus 30 cents an hour for cleaning up the fire hall or practising — a spokesman felt obliged to defend such extravagance:

"This may seem like good pay but many of the members (of the department) could testify to the loss they have sustained through damage of clothing, especially by responding to alarms on the Sabbath when they have on their store clothes to go to see their best girl."

The 7th Ave. fire hall itself caused a considerable flare-up. It cost $125 and the furnishings, particularly the chairs, were a lot more comfortable than anything available at the city hall. So the town council began holding its meetings in the fire hall. The firemen were furious, and the whole force turned in its resignation.

Fine, said the mayor, he and the aldermen would form their own fire department. The arrangement lasted until the next fire broke out, and the council proved hopelessly inept in coping with it. The council moved out of the fire hall and the firemen moved back in.

James "Cappy" Smart, born in Arbroath, Scotland, in 1865, emerged on the local scene as a fire captain in 1891. He became the fire chief in 1898 and headed the department in his own inimitable way until 1933.

Cappy Smart figured the place for the chief to be at any fire was in the middle of the smoke and water. Smoke, it was said, made him swear. If onlookers pressed in too closely, his answer was to turn the hoses on them.

This practice applied to everybody, regardless of whether they had a vested interest in the fire. One woman whose house was on fire persisted in standing there ranting about how the firemen were too slow getting to the scene. Cappy, in his customary fashion, shut her up by turning the hoses on her.

The firemen's hockey, lacrosse, rugby, baseball, football, boxing and snowshoeing teams were greatly respected by opponents. Cappy Smart was president of the Exhibition Board and Stampede parade marshall. He played in the fire department band and refereed all local boxing

James 'Cappy' Smart, 1865-1939.

matches. If the match was important enough, he appeared in evening dress.

The department's May 24 sports day, St. Patrick's Day party and Firemen's Ball were major social events. The firemen's brass band won prizes in competitions all over the place. And they had political clout. It was said that a candidate didn't have much chance of getting elected to office if the firemen didn't like him.

With the passing of time the department acquired new equipment and sophistication. In 1973, even the traditional red fire engines were abandoned. The replacements are lemon-lime, fluorescent machines that shine in the dark.

It was a sad day in December, 1973, when they abandoned the old No. 1 fire hall on 6th Ave. and moved into a sparkling, but hardly historic, new building two blocks north. With all its sentimental significance, the old hall, opened in 1911, was plain worn out.

Historical significance notwithstanding, the move no doubt was a good idea. The new structure is built of concrete, Gyproc and metal. The old brick building had a wooden interior. It would have been a supreme embarrassment if the old hall had burned down while the firemen were still in it.

The Calgary fire brigade in 1887.

The home front

Soldiers stage a mock battle on the North Hill during the Second World War.

Far from any major (or minor) theatres of war, Calgary scarcely thinks of itself as a military base. Eighth Ave. ends abruptly at the front door of Mewata Armories, viewed by some as a bastion of the military presence, by others as an architectural monstrosity. On 17th Ave., far from any ocean, there's a land-locked battleship called Tecumseh. At the entrance to Calgary International Airport, a Lancaster bomber recalls the Second World War. Even that now seems a long time ago.

Yet Calgary still is, officially, a garrison city. "Our" boys still go to war, though it's a lot different from the way it once was. The troops who go to war are a permanent force, not part-time reservists. From time to time they are called away to stand between warring factions in such far-away places as Korea, Vietnam, Cyprus, or the Middle East.

The Calgary garrison is a city within a city. Centred at Currie Barracks and Camp Sarcee, it sprawls over a large part of southwestern Calgary and beyond into the Sarcee Reserve. East of Crowchild Trail, the permanent married quarters streets bear such evocative names as Somme Crescent, Vimy Drive, Amiens St., and Korea Ave.

Today, for most Calgarians, war is something they read about or see, in fleeting glimpses, on their tv screens. There have been times when the city's commitment was much more direct — and unquestioned. Militarily, Calgary has traditions second to none. Along with an annual squabble about whether the stores should close, they are commemorated each year on Remembrance Day.

Who could really explain today why someone from here would rush off to South Africa to fight the Boers at the turn of the century? Actually, the answer is simple enough. It was Britain's war. This was an integral part of the British Empire. That was sufficient.

Much the same applies to 1914, when the First World War caused Calgary's young men to fight and die in France and Belgium. A Calgary Herald editorial in August, 1914, is worth quoting at length because it sums up so graphically the emotions that prevailed then.

"That success will crown our banners no Britisher doubts," The Herald proclaimed, "for God is with the right. The star of Britain's empire, which has lit the path of civilization for a thousand years, will shine all the more brightly once these clouds are past.

"Great Britain's part in the general upheaval is clear. As mistress of the seas and the world's most powerful nation in diplomacy, and all that makes for world peace and betterment, her duty will be to punish to the limit of her ability the trouble-makers of Europe and the world generally — Germany and Austria. The arrogance and intolerance of the Teuton ruling house must be once and for all checked if human progress is to continue as it should, and to Great Britain falls the weighty portion of the task of administering the rebuke and corrective.

"Britain's sons everywhere are ready to do and to die if necessary. There will be no flinching, no hesitating."

At the same time Britain's sons were admonished to remember other things:

"One is to treat with courtesy and moderation residents in our midst who happen to belong to the nationalities with which our country is at war. There are in Calgary some thousands of these people, and a similar proportion probably exists in other western countries. They came to Canada at our invitation, they have made their homes with us and have been and are good citizens; they are non-belligerants; they occupy the tragical position of being forcibly resident in a foreign and unfriendly country."

The warning was timely, but it went unheeded. Minority groups were neither understood nor appreciated. In the heat of war, intense nationalistic passions boiled over.

The outbreak of the first war was announced

Calgary parade late in First World War; face masks were common during flu epidemic.

in moving picture and vaudeville houses, where house orchestras played rousing renditions of Rule Britannia and The Marseillaise. Ulstermen who, meeting in the Orange Hall, had just voted to "take up arms" for Ulster in the event of trouble in Ireland, found themselves off target. The real menace in 1914 was Kaiser Bill.

There was a great rush to enlist at the old 103rd Armories, east of Centre St. near the river. Then the troops marched off to the CPR depot, and everybody cheered them on their way. A pure milk depot was organized, the objective being more and better milk so Calgary could produce more and better babies. How this would aid the war effort is a bit unclear.

Everybody figured the war would be over in six months. The theatres were thriving: "Kitty MacKay will open Grand Theatre," "Bright Musical Sketch at Pantages," "Francis X. Bushman at Regent today." The task of building Mewata Armories wouldn't be started until later. Ironically, it was completed in 1918.

A department store advertised "Rule Britannia Flag Day." Five thousand flags were to be given away to children accompanied by adults. Also available were "several tables of toys you will like. Prices are very, very low. Have fun. Boys can be soldiers and the girls nurses, and you can play at real war."

When it became evident that the real war was going to last a lot longer than six months, the jollity that attended initial preparations to fight it disappeared. The boys overseas were being killed, and the mood on the home front turned ugly.

On the night of Feb. 16, 1916, a mob of 500, mostly soldiers quartered at Sarcee and Victoria Park, wrecked the White Lunch at 128 8th Ave. S.E., then demolished a dance hall above it. The cause of the riot was a rumor that the manager had fired an ex-soldier and hired an Austrian in his place.

The next night, a mixed mob of 1,500 soldiers and civilians demolished the furniture, the bar and the windows of the Riverside Hotel at the north end of the Langevin Bridge. Looters strolled the streets with bottles in their pockets and boxes of cigars under their arms. The justification was that the hotel was "owned by a German."

The city was on the verge of mob rule. Mayor M. C. Costello appealed on the front page of The Herald for people to stay off the streets. A military inquiry resulted in bars being temporarily ruled

Riverside Hotel after 1916 riot.

off limits to soldiers. A degree of sanity eventually was restored.

To single out any one unit among those that served overseas would be to omit another equally deserving. Suffice it to say that Calgary's hastily-mobilized volunteers acquitted themselves with irrefutable distinction. The record speaks for itself.

At home, jubilation was unrestrained on Nov. 11, 1918. Armistice Day. The war was over. The Calgary Canadian, one of the local newspapers of the day, reported as follows:

"If it were possible for any other city in the allied world to fail in its duty in celebrating the great and glorious news of peace, then Calgary certainly made up for any lack. Celebrations began with word of peace at 2 a.m. on Monday morning, and ran 24 hours.

"Everybody worked like Trojans getting up the decorations, and in devising every possible scheme they could think of to make a noise. The louder the noise the better. From early morn to dewey eve and far into the night the noise of the celebrations rose into the air.

"Long before noon all the downtown stores were completely sold out of fireworks. Then the mob descended on Chinatown, where the wideawake Chinks did a roaring business."

The author of this obviously thought nothing of referring to the residents of Chinatown as Chinks.

A wagon loaded with "socks for Tommy" outside newspaper office in 1916.

He was more concerned about how hard it was to work with people ringing cow-bells in his ear:

"All there was to do was to get out and cheer and make a noise and shake hands with everyone and congratulate everyone, for everyone knew everyone else."

An effigy of Germany's Kaiser swung in the wind outside The Canadian's office. Passersby stopped and shook a fist at it. Then "a torch was applied to the figures of the Beast of Berlin and his degenerate son, the Clown Prince (sic)." There was a parade, and bonfires on Mount Royal and Crescent Heights. Church bells pealed. Owners of new autos honked their horns.

The war to end all wars bought two decades of peace. Normalcy never quite returned to Calgary. First there was the facade of the Roaring '20s, then the Dirty '30s. In 1939, seeds of discontent sown in Europe 20 years earlier gave birth to the Second World War.

This time, Canada underlined its independence by waiting a few days after Britain declared war before following suit. But the results

were the same. The issue was clear-cut, and again Calgarians were among the first and most enthusiastic to enlist.

The war came at a time when the country was quietly staggering back from the depression. The wheat crop in 1939 was the biggest in 10 years. Wheat remained important to the war effort, but other matters took precedence.

Wooden barracks were hurriedly erected along the southeast side of Mewata Armories. Shacks and tents sprouted on the Sarcee Reserve. The militia, comprising those too old, too young, or otherwise unable to go overseas, trained there. Many still living here will remember those tents with mixed emotions.

A mounted constabulary was organized to protect dams, electrical installations and bridges. The army issued saddles, bridles, blankets and 30.30 Winchesters, but the volunteers had to provide their own horses, feed and grooms. They would work at their regular jobs all day, then, as required, often ride patrol all night. With its horses and riders the constabulary was, in its fashion, a fitting way for the old cowtown to handle home defence.

Soldiers bound for Second World War duty leave Calgary station.

Gas rationing in the war years led one Calgary firm to institute the "horsemobile".

The Commonwealth Air Training Plan brought trainees here from all over the world. In the wide-open spaces over Calgary, High River, Claresholm and Penhold they found ideal flying conditions. Individual airmen were "adopted" by local families, and it was the start of many life-long friendships. Many from overseas came back here to live after the war. Some married local girls. Another contribution was adding the name "Paralyzer" for the Palliser to the local vocabulary.

The combination of Commonwealth service men taking Calgary to heart while thousands of Calgary men served overseas, returning after 1945, gave the city a new cosmopolitanism. The previous generation had discovered English pubs. This generation rediscovered them — and also came back with a new appreciation for fine wine.

By 1940 the patriotic fashion in clothing was an armed forces uniform. Under the National Registration Act, more than 67,000 individuals here were named, numbered, and checked out. It wasn't conscription. The government just wanted to know where everybody was and what he was doing.

Stimulated by oratory, military parades and bands, the first War Savings bond drive was quickly oversubscribed. The casualty lists started coming in, and a telegram often was something to be dreaded. Unemployment was dropping, but rationing began and housing was scarce.

An internment camp for "enemy" aliens — Germans and Italians — was established at Kananaskis. Later in the war, it served as a prisoner-of-war camp. There was much consterna-

A Calgary Store owner explains that blue ration tokens are needed for that Sunday roast.

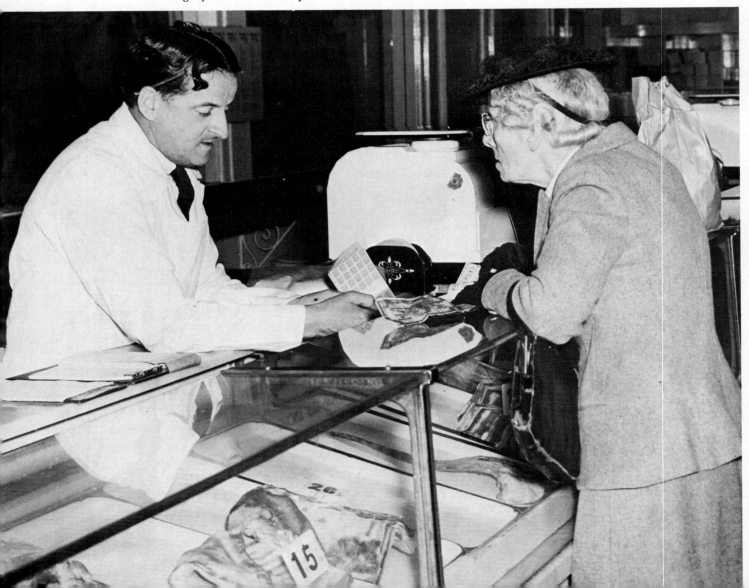

tion when someone escaped, as happened quite often.

Hundreds of young farmers went overseas. Surprisingly, it was discovered they made fine sailors as well as soldiers. But they left a shortage of help to bring in continuing good harvests. The situation was worse during the First World War, when farms weren't mechanized, but it still was a problem in the Second World War.

A call went out for help from the cities. Among others, an enthusiastic but hopelessly inept crew from The Calgary Herald's news room rushed to the rescue. Knowing nothing about farming, they wound up behind the stooks drinking beer. They were useless, but they meant well. Everybody did.

Some street and display lights in the city were dimmed in an attempt to conserve power. One or two attempts were made to practise total blackouts, but it was hard to convince anyone that the Luftwaffe was anywhere near. Some people shaded their windows, and that was about it.

Two records were noted in 1943. The Calgary bull sale grossed $250,000. And Christmas mail overseas reached unprecedented proportions. Prominent in the outgoing mail were "ditty bags" for Calgary sailors fighting German U-boats. Typically they contained chocolate, warm hats, gloves, or anything else a sailor on the cold North Atlantic run might need.

In June 1944, the Allied forces landed in Normandy. A D-Day crowd numbering in the

It's over, and men of the 1st Canadian Infantry Brigade march proudly through the streets of Calgary before cheering thousands.

At the CPR station.

thousands gathered at 7th Ave. and 1st St. S.W. for prayers.

The coffee and tea ration was lifted that year, and there even was some ammunition available for hunters. The Red Cross opened a reception centre for returning wounded at the CPR depot.

Except for too many homes where a telegram arrived advising that a loved one was dead, wounded or missing, rationing and shortages were the most visible evidence that the city was at war. Meatless Tuesdays, and later Meatless Fridays, were observed in local restaurants and hotels, starting in 1943.

Ration books, first introduced in 1942, at various times limited purchases of meat, coffee, tea, sugar and butter. A total of 102,891 ration books covering everyone down to the youngest child were issued in the Calgary district in January, 1944. Gasoline also was rationed. Permits were required for liquor and beer.

Acquiring liquor permits became a fine art. The low point was reached in April, 1944. Individuals were allowed 13 ounces of liquor a month, 26 ounces of wine a month, 6 large or 12 small bottles of beer a week. Military messes fared better, but the quota at local golf clubs was a dismal 10 small bottles of beer per member per month.

Due to the sugar shortage, housewives were discouraged from putting up preserves. The maximum allowance in 1943 was six fluid ounces of jams and jellies, and 10 ounces of canned fruit. Much indignation attended the discovery that a citizen was hoarding sugar in his basement.

The meat ration in May, 1943, averaged out at about two pounds per person per week. Farmers weren't exempt. They had to turn in coupons covering any meat they slaughtered. If they helped out needy neighbors, they had to collect coupons and receipts.

Customers in restaurants got limited amounts of butter and sugar only if they asked for it. Everything was in short supply, from automobile tires to silk stockings, corsets and girdles. Nightgowns, it was decreed, could not exceed 52 inches in length. Double-breasted suits and cuffs on trousers were banned.

Victory in Europe was celebrated May 8, 1945, and Victory in Japan on Aug. 15. Christmas, 1945, was proclaimed as "the happiest holiday." Some families were reunited for Christmas for the first time since 1938.

The twin victories were celebrated locally with parades, bonfires, and cheering crowds in the streets. There were complaints about too much noise, exuberance "and some property damage by crowds of teen-agers," but it wasn't too serious. English "war brides" began arriving in Calgary, completing the cosmopolitan circle started by the overseas airmen stationed here earlier.

Rationing finally ended Nov. 3, 1947. Sugar, the first food item to be rationed (in September, 1942), was the last to be set free. Housewives finally could throw away the little multi-colored coupon booklet that had been their constant shopping companion for five years.

Such inconveniences were as nothing compared to the tragedies of war casualties and the anxieties of those with families in the war zones, but they were universal, touching everybody.

In the late '50s and early '60s, when the Cold War was threatening to turn hot, there was a brief rush to build fallout shelters. There still are some old shelters in some Calgary basements, abandoned now to the realization that they likely wouldn't be much use if there's ever another time around.

Get-up-and-go times

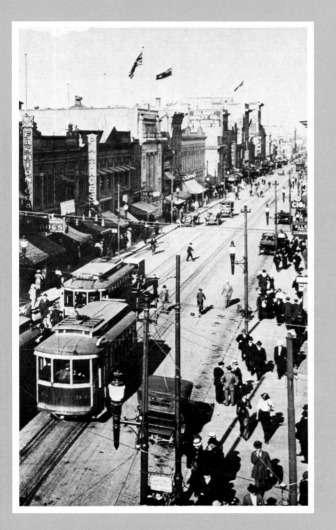

A glance at the map shows how Calgary is surrounded by mostly nothing at all. Beyond the city limits there's bald-faced prairie or mostly-vacant foothills country. A trip to the next major city in any direction involves long-distance travelling.

Getting from one place to another within the 155.8 square miles encompassed by the city limits also can be no mean feat. It's about 10 miles from Bowness in the west to Forest Lawn in the east, 14 miles from Huntington Hills in the north to Midnapore in the south.

The biggest jumbo jets now land and take off from here regularly on a 12,675-foot runway, the longest commercial runway in Canada. For many today, the world is only a custom's check away. London, England, is only eight hours from Calgary via a direct, non-stop flight.

Yet the town is so young that not so very much time has passed, really, since the era of the stage coach, the Red River cart, and the bull-whackers on the Whoop-Up Trail. For half its history Calgary was a horse town. But never a one-horse town, please — F Troop originally arrived here with 50 horses.

Passengers on the early stage-coach runs didn't get martinis or a small steak in a platter along the way. They were happy just to get where they wanted to go. They didn't really expect to be held up, but it did happen once. The image of the Wild West probably would lack something without at least one such instance of dastardly derring-do.

On Aug. 23, 1886, the Edmonton stage, with a full complement of passengers, was 18 miles out of

Early street cars rumble through downtown Calgary in 1909.

The Calgary-to-Edmonton stage coach in the 1890s.

Calgary when two bandits sprang from hiding in the tall grass. Waving carbines and revolvers, they relieved driver Pete Campbell of $200, ransacked the mail bags and luggage, unhitched the horses, and galloped north. Pete and his passengers trudged glumly back to Calgary.

The outlaws were never caught. The only clue was that they seemed to be good, patriotic lads. Their masks were crudely manufactured from a Union Jack flag.

The railway put the stage coaches out of business. And the romanticists, if not always the passengers, had a love affair with trains that lasted from 1886, when the first trans-continental steamed through here, until they retired the big mountain-climbing 5900 locomotives. One of the last of the

5900s still can be seen at Mewata Park. The diesels that replaced them never had the same pizzaz.

The old locomotives, from the basic-black, bell-ringing wood burners to the mountain-gobbling giants, had a personality the diesels lack. Each bore a number, not a name, but railroaders knew them individually. There was something about the way each of them grunted, gurgled and rumbled.

In the old days, to discover the land beyond the next hill was adventure enough. The prairies were vast, the mountains mysterious, and the railway spanned them both. The seats might be harder, the window sills dirtier, and the pace more tedious, but the romance was there.

The 5900s were masters of the Rocky and Selkirk ranges from 1929 until the early 1950s. The CPR owned 35 in the 5900 series. They were known as Selkirks, and they were the biggest locomotives in the Commonwealth. They were oil burners, 98 feet long, weighing 447,000 pounds fully loaded with oil and water. They were magnificent beasts, conjuring visions of power over the longest distance or the highest hill.

Nobody goes down to the tracks any more to watch the train come in, and to wave to the crew and passengers. Anyway, the railway would rather pack freight. It pays better and it doesn't talk back.

Pioneer historian Leroy Kelly recorded in 1912 how hitching-posts in front of the hotels had given way to automobiles. Stock men were unhappy in 1912 because the railway claimed 18 miles per hour

The Prince family with the team and buggy in front of the Peter Prince home in 1896.

This hydrogen-filled airship made 5 successful flights over Calgary for the Dominion exhibition in 1908.

was the best its stock trains could do on the main line. But the U.S. lines seemed to have no trouble making 25 miles per hour. Maybe even more.

The first automobile appeared in Calgary in 1903, driven by rancher W. F. Cochrane. It's said that when Cochrane first drove his car over his ranch land, a cowboy thought the fool thing was out of control and tried to lasso it.

Charlie Jackson, the town's first milk man, later bought Cochrane's oddity, a steam-propelled Locomobile, and kept it going for 30 years. For

Charlie Jackson and the first milk wagon in 1884-85.

many years a featured attraction in the Stampede parade, it's now preserved for posterity in the Glenbow Museum.

Peter Prince and his brother John acquired a gas-driven Rambler in 1904. R. B. Bennett had an Oldsmobile and Calgary Herald editor J. J. Young drove a McLaughlin in 1905. Lacking experience behind the wheel, Bennett drove his one-cylinder machine up the pavement and into the side of the Imperial Bank on Stephen Ave. After that he employed a chauffeur.

Bob Edwards, a pedestrian, commented from the sidelines that normally "the first thing a man with a new automobile runs into is debt."

A photo of the Prince machine shows a wide-open two-seater with the engine plainly in view and the steering wheel jutting up at a sharp angle. All the early cars were open cars. If it rained, the driver could put up the top and button on side curtains that he carried beneath the seat cushion.

The early autos were alarming, particularly to horses. Grant MacEwan has recorded an early list of alleged rules designed to control them. That such a list would be drafted by horse men, not car owners, seems self-evident:

1. When an approaching team (of horses) is observed the automobilist must stop offside and

cover his machine with a tarpaulin painted to correspond with the scenery.

2. A driver approaching a corner where he cannot command a view of all incoming roads must stop not less than 100 yards from the turn and toot his horn before proceeding.

3. Penalty for speeding, $1 for every mile per hour over 10.

4. In case of autos making horses run away the compensation to the horseowner will be $50 for the first mile the horses run, $100 the second mile, in addition to customary charges.

Rules such as these were never actually enforced, and the car had pretty much replaced the horse by the 1920s. There still were some horses around during the '20s, mostly working in drays with heavy loads. One stable on 17th Ave. survived into the 1940s.

Long before this, however, both horses and cars were almost literally pushed off the street by another astonishing phenomenon, the Calgary Municipal Railway.

In 1908, the city council called tenders for 16 miles of street railway track and 12 cars. Mayor R. R. Jamieson promised to have electric cars on the streets for the opening of the Provincial Exhibition in July, 1909. The first two cars arrived from the factory 48 hours before the deadline.

Puffed with pride and pancakes, mayor and aldermen turned out at 8 a.m. for the inaugural ride from the Alberta Hotel to Victoria Park. A large crowd cheered the two-car procession on its way. The Calgary Daily News reported:

"They travelled at a fairly good speed down the main street and made the grade at the Second Street subway successfully."

During Exhibition Week, the two cars carried 35,500 passengers, many of them riding back and forth for the novelty of it. Then the politicians blundered. The city councillors voted themselves free passes. The resolution of the issue isn't recorded, but a civic furore of the type that isn't

Peter and John Prince go for a spin around Calgary in their Rambler auto in 1904.

A family outing in 1906: even on Mission Hill, there were rules to be followed.

altogether uncommon today ensued. Particularly embittered, because they didn't get any free passes, were the commissioners and civic employees.

The early street-car system was a menace to life and limb. One tram on the North Hill run would skid off the tracks and into a store on 4th St. N.E. with notorious regularity. Another heading downhill at 17th Ave. and 14th St. S.W. failed to make the turn at the bottom and plowed into a drug store.

But the Calgary Municipal Railway was here to stay. By July 5, 1910, the system had 18 cars operating over 22 miles of track. In 1911, the rail lines were extended to serve all of Crescent Heights and the CPR's Ogden Shops. And Bowness became "the town a street car built."

English-born developer John Hextall owned hundreds of acres of range land in Bowness, and he was a builder. His mansion later became Wood's Christian Home. He built the Shouldice Bridge and that monument to gracious golfing, the Bowness Golf and Country Club. For Bowness itself he visualized a model town, "the suburb perfect."

His problem in 1911 was that, situated away out in the middle of nowhere, his holdings weren't worth much. The solution was an ingenious deal between Hextall and the Calgary Municipal Railway. The railway acquired scenic Bowness Park in exchange for a commitment to build a street railway line to Hextall's home. In 1912, the first tram ran literally up to his doorstep.

The Bowness run was a local institution from 1912 until it was abandoned in April, 1950. The line ran through wide-open country. The tram's headlight could be seen poking and swaying across the open range at night. Fun-seekers from Calgary travelled by tram to Bowness, and the car returned daily with fresh milk from the Springbank dairy farm. The popularity of the park proved more enduring than the rail link that gave it birth.

From 1913 to 1930, the showpiece of the street railway system was the Rubberneck Special. An observation car with a gaily decorated canvas top, open sides, sloping deck seats and plate glass mirrors along the sides, the Special was a magnetic attraction for both local sightseers and tourists.

The electric-powered Special completed two scenic tours of the city daily. Each tour lasted one hour. A conductor with a megaphone extolled each passing attraction. The fare was 25 cents.

Calgary's last street car traversed the Ogden run Dec. 29, 1950, then gave way to a modern fleet of rubber-tired electric trolley coaches and gasoline or diesel-powered motor buses. At last count, the Calgary Transit System operated 85 trolleys and 208 motor or diesel buses on 31 routes over 451 miles. The first route, from downtown to Victoria Park, was half a mile.

Aviation in Calgary dates back to about 1906. A newspaper account that year records that Prof. Williams, otherwise unidentified, went up in a hot-air balloon at the Exhibition. He jumped out twice, landing (1) in the Elbow River and (2) on the ground.

Dominion Day, 1911, and an outing to Bowness Park was made even more exciting by having the passengers get out and push.

The clang, clang (and clunk) of the trolley

An interior view of Calgary's first street car, taken in 1909. Mayor R. R. Jamieson, third from left, rides with the city commissioners and railway superintendent.

A street car failed to make the turn at 14th St. and 17th Ave. S.W. in 1919.

The Rubberneck Special sets out for a one-hour tour of the city.

A history of aviation in Calgary was compiled in 1962 by John Gladstone, of the aircraft maintenance technology department, Southern Alberta Institute of Technology. He records that the first attempt to fly a heavier-than-air machine here was made in 1906 by two young boys.

They built "a kite-like affair" powered by a one-cylinder motorcycle engine. A two-cylinder Buick towed this affair along the Bowness Trail, and it flew for about 30 or 40 feet in the air.

In October, 1911, The Herald sponsored what was called the city's first "aviation meet." A U.S. pilot was hired to come here and demonstrate a biplane. At altitudes up to 2,000 feet he flew directly over the city centre, landing in the exhibition grounds.

Katherine Stinson, a famous U.S. woman pilot, was hired to do three stunt flights daily at the 1916 Exhibition. Two years later she was hired by the Edmonton Exhibition. En route north, she stopped in Calgary, picked up a bag of mail containing 259 letters, and delivered it in Edmonton amid much fanfare. It was the first air-mail flight for both cities.

The First World War really got aviation off the ground and, much later, Calgary's McCall Field is well named. Frederick Robert Gordon McCall was Canada's fourth-ranked air ace. Serving with the Royal Flying Corps, he accounted for 37 enemy planes.

Some of his home-front exploits were equally hair-raising. In 1919, he was stunt flying over the exhibition grounds with two young sons of the exhibition manager as passengers. His engine failed while an auto race was in progress on the track below. Heading for the midway, he crash-landed in the middle of an operating merry-go-round. No one was hurt.

Freddy McCall founded the first Calgary-based aircraft company, McCall Aero Corporation Limited, in 1919, and the Calgary Aero Club in 1927. In 1928, he flew (carefully) 200 quarts of nitroglycerine from Montana to Calgary. He served in the Second World War, survived that, too, and died in 1949.

Calgary's first airfields were scattered around the west end in Bowness and Wildwood, near the present Sarcee Trail and the Banff Coach Road. Privately owned, they often were plagued by wind currents over the Bow River. Early pilots often

Freddy McCall in the cockpit of a Tiger Moth in 1939.

landed wherever they could, regardless of where the airport was supposed to be. It probably wasn't much of an airport anyway.

There was plenty of available space. The first municipal airport, inaugurated Sept. 12, 1929, was south of the present Trans-Canada Highway in the Renfrew district. "Calgary's air fleet" had its picture taken to mark the occasion. The fleet consisted of 10 prop-driven monoplanes and biplanes.

In 1930, a 60-foot steel beacon was erected on top of the Hudson's Bay Company store. One of the first aeronautical beacons in the world, it consisted of a 3-million candle power beam pointing toward the airport and a battery of red lights visible 150 miles away.

The first airport at the present site was opened just prior to the Second World War. "International" status was slow in coming. Trans-Canada Air Lines' main cross-country run touched down at Lethbridge, not Calgary. The Crow's Nest Pass was considered to be the easiest and safest route over the mountains.

Today the Calgary International Airport ranks fourth in Canada in total numbers of passengers arriving, departing, or waiting for late flights. A new, $80 million terminal is scheduled for completion in 1976. Or maybe 1977. With further expansion, in four planned stages, it theoretically will meet all future needs until the year 2001.

In July 1919, his engine stalled, and with no other place to land, McCall chose the midway. No one was hurt.

Aviation yesterday and today. Top photo shows Katherine Stinson as she picks up the mail for the first air mail flight to Edmonton in 1918. Below, the scene today at the Calgary International Airport where jets take off minutes apart on the nation's longest commercial runway.

A bankrupt land

Unemployed drifters in 1931.

The overseas wars shaped the attitudes and outlook of many who survived them for the rest of their lives. The most traumatic peacetime experience here — everywhere, in fact — was the Great Depression of the 1930s.

The stage was set during the 1920s, a considerably misunderstood decade. The Roaring Twenties was mainly a U.S. invention made up of about equal parts of fact and fancy. Calgary didn't do much roaring. Construction was at a near standstill. Wages from 1920 to 1929 rose about 10 to 15 per cent. Today that's about par for a single year.

For something to cheer about during both the '20s and the '30s, Calgary relied on recurring oil booms in Turner Valley. During the 1920s, people gambled on everything from oil and wheat to slot machines (until they were declared illegal). The atmosphere was confident but speculative, and rampant over-speculation toppled the whole fiscal edifice in October, 1929.

Significantly for the political future of the province, Alberta got caught specifically in a vicious cycle of prices, debts, and interest. Post-war inflation, the high cost of mechanizing farms, high interest rates and boom-bust-boom grain prices preceded the over-all collapse, and set people to looking for a better way to do business.

Years of drought coincided with the collapse of the money system. What was it like out there on the farms? There are photos enough showing the desolation. But Calgary Herald columnist Ken Liddell, in a remarkable feat of recollection 40 years later, remembered the sound, not the sight, of the depression. It was the wind:

"There would be with us today, a generation and even better, who would have no knowledge of it except by hearsay. But to those who do remember it, the memory is not so much the sight of the land, but the symphony of the wind, an orchestration that cursed each day, day after day, for weeks on end.

"It would die, occasionally, toward sundown to make night a blessed relief from the agonizing moans of some unseen and powerful monster that literally tore the guts out of the land and its people, an enemy which man could neither trap nor tame.

"You couldn't breathe without choking. You couldn't talk without screaming. You couldn't see without blinking to protect the eyes from pellets of dust. Humans took to wearing goggles. They could do nothing but listen to the weird, mind-numbing song of the wind, a sound that could be neither duplicated nor forgotten, once heard."

In the city, goods remained plentiful and prices were at a rock-bottom low. Some fared comparatively well during the depression. Anyone who had saved $500 or so during the '20s was well off, as was anyone who could hold onto a job paying $25 a week during the '30s.

But they were the exceptions. Farmers, the unemployed, people coming onto the job market and finding no jobs, and investors who went broke in 1929 had no way of fending for themselves.

There were no jobs, no money, no demand for goods and services.

Carl Nickle, now a successful oil man, remembers finishing school in 1935 and going to work in a shoe store for $14 a week. Times got tougher, and the owner of the store fired his shoe-shine boy. Carl sold shoes, and shined them, for $12 a week.

Then the owner of the store had to let his repair man go. He wanted Carl to sell shoes, shine them, and repair them for $10 a week. Carl quit, went on relief, and worked on the Trans-Canada Highway near Cochrane.

John Hextall's development lots in Bowness, valued at $1,500 in 1911, sold for $100 in the 1930s. There weren't many buyers at any price.

The depression was a great equalizer. Senator Ernest Manning, then crusading for Social Credit across arid southern Alberta, remembers the friendliness and hospitality of everybody he met. His new-style politics offered people something to do and a chance to get involved in seeking answers to their problems.

No money for gas, farmers resorted to the "Bennett Buggy", like this one on an Alberta farm.

A dust storm sweeps across the parched land at Fort Macleod.

Lacking money, people tried to make their own fun. Political rallies, "socials" and dances all drew crowds. There's a story about a lad who went to all the local dances with a $20 bill. He never paid because no one ever could change a $20 bill.

The city operated a soup kitchen under the old grandstand at Victoria Park. The Stampede reserved a block of seats in its new concrete grandstand for "registered unemployed and their families." The horse-racing season was short: a $2 bet was a serious investment. All forms of sports were avidly pursued for the brief respite they offered from the drab sameness of depression life.

In 1932, a Calgary lawyer estimated that the price of wheat, being $9 a ton, was less than the price of sawdust, which was $10 a ton. Toronto Globe and Mail columnist Richard J. Needham, former chief editorial writer for The Herald, checked in with this recollection of Calgary in 1936:

"What with the dust, drought, depression and debt, the city — the whole province, the whole West — was on its uppers. Auntie Ottawa was buying up cattle for one cent a pound, and kindly church congregations in Ontario were sending carloads of vegetables and used clothing to the Western peasantry, thereby earning their life-long ingratitude."

Regular air-mail service between Calgary and Winnipeg, inaugurated in 1930, was abandoned because it was too costly in 1931. Farmers managed to bring in a decent crop in 1932, but the bottom fell out of grain prices. A hard winter left the cattle industry nearly bankrupt.

The worst depression years in Calgary were between 1932 and 1936. The CPR closed down its shops. The 1933 grain crop, beset by drought, hail, wind, grasshoppers, rust and frost, was minuscule. The railroad used snow ploughs to clear the tracks of soil drifts 10 feet high.

Senator Harry Hays remembers that in 1934 the Hays Farm employed 18 men, nine working for $25 a month and nine for only their board. They hauled milk from the farm to the city in a truck. Then they couldn't afford the truck any more, and went back to using horse-drawn vehicles.

He recalls taking nine heifers to the stockyards on a Monday morning. The stockyards phoned on Friday to say no one wanted to buy them. Mr. Hays

A wheel-barrow brigade, made up of relief workers,
at work in the Bankview area of Calgary in 1931.

A wrestling class was held at the YMCA for unemployed men in 1935.

got them back and shot them. The following Wednesday he received a bill for $11 for feed. He took cattle to Scotland and sold them by auction. With expenses deducted, the net loss was $10 a head.

Here are some typical prices quoted by Calgary retail stores between 1932 and 1935:

Sirloin or T-bone roasts or steaks, 18 cents a pound; chuck roasts, 10 cents a pound; bacon, 10 cents a pound; minced steak, 6 cents a pound; beef sausage, 6 cents a pound; potatoes, 10 pounds for 19 cents; sugar, 10 pounds for 62 cents; eggs, two dozen for 25 cents; can of pork and beans, 5 cents.

Wool, tweed and serge men's suits were advertised for $9.95, extra pants $3. Snap-brim straw hats sold for $1. Hotel rooms were advertised at $1 to $2 per night. Monthly rates were lower. For anyone who could afford it, Jasper Park Lodge charged $7 a day and up with meals.

Steak dinners could be had in restaurants for 25 cents. Recreation might consist of a day at the Calgary Zoo or even a day in the public library. A movie was an occasional luxury. Admissions in 1932 ranged up to 25 cents. Matinee prices were a bit lower.

Teachers were in demand for multi-grade classes in district schools. They could expect to earn about $600 a year, perhaps more if they had special qualifications. In 1935, miners in Drumheller estimated their take-home pay had dropped 40 per cent since 1924.

B.C. author and journalist Barry Broadfoot collected the personal recollections of Canadian survivors of the depression and compiled them in a book called *Ten Lost Years*. Here are three vignettes that involved Calgary:

A farm hand walking home stopped at a small farm and bought four dozen eggs, two pounds of butter, six good-sized onions, sliced-up chard leaves and five loaves of bread. The total price, which the farm family was delighted to get, was 50 cents. Mixed up in a wash-pan and devoured by a crew of farm workers, the concoction was celebrated locally as "the famous Calgary omelette".

An old lady called Mother Melville would go down to "the jungle on the Bow River" with a purse full of stamped envelopes and sheets of paper. "Write your mother, son," she would exhort the

hobos there. And 15 or 20 hobos would pass a pencil around, writing home.

A fairly well-to-do Calgary church sponsored White Gift Sundays prior to Christmas. Children were asked to bring a gift for the poor — anything useful — wrapped in white tissue paper. In 1934-35 it was noticed that many of the packages were empty. The poor were in the congregation. Asked to contribute something worth about 50 cents, they just didn't have the money.

In 1932, a $235,000 bylaw to build the 4th St. W. subway was defeated by 4,093 to 1,918. It was the biggest "no" vote on a money bylaw in the city's history.

A Calgary book and stationery store advertised

Bargains abounded in the depression — if you had the money. This ad ran in The Herald on May 10, 1935 and perhaps typified an era.

Calgary's United Married Men's Association staged a march on behalf of "12,000 men on relief" in 1935.

In June 1932, the Bow River flooded a good part of the Sunnyside area of Calgary.

a close-out sale ("*I'm through! Take it away! Prices blasted to blazes*") for weeks on end.

Families on relief received vouchers for food, fuel and rent. In 1935, the city adopted a "work for wages" plan. Employable heads of families on relief were allowed to work it out at 45 cents an hour, the advantage being that they could receive cash in place of vouchers.

City relief crews worked on road graveling and grading, sewer laying, and straightening the Banff highway inside the city limits. Provincial relief crews planted 12,000 trees on the grounds of the Technical Institute on the North Hill.

Radio, which got a foothold here in the 1920s, played a unique role throughout the 1930s. For those without work or money, it was virtually the only form of entertainment available.

An early aviator and "wireless" operator, W. W. Grant brought radio to Calgary in 1922. His first broadcast, from High River, was picked up by The Calgary Herald's new radio station (later CFAC) in a tiny studio in the old Greyhound Building.

Grant moved to Calgary and opened another station the same year. This one became CFCN, the late H. Gordon Love's "Voice of The Prairies," reaching from B.C. to Saskatchewan. In the early 1930s, CFCN carried William Aberhart's first broadcasts.

Relief work programs organized by the federal, provincial and municipal governments inevitably bred discontent. There inevitably were clashes between the unemployed, the relief workers and the law.

Mounted police fought demonstrators in what was known as "Red Square," an intersection near the present public library. On 4th St. south of 26th Ave., police fought disillusioned relief gangs in what came to be known as the Battle of Mission Hill. Almost always, "Communist agitators" were blamed for the violence.

It was R. B. Bennett's misfortune that Calgary chose this time to provide Canada with a prime minister.

Richard Bedford Bennett had been prominent in every aspect of Calgary life for years — while never quite managing to look as if he really belonged here. Many remember him as being fair-minded and meticulously honest. It's even said he had a sense of humor. But he managed to keep it well hidden beneath his immaculate morning coat and wing collar or frock coat and top hat.

Richard Bedford Bennett: he gave his own money to the poor, but he couldn't win them over.

Henry Wise Wood.

Reputedly, he decided as a young boy that he was going to become prime minister of Canada. Arriving in Calgary from the Maritimes in 1897, he didn't waste any time. He was elected to the Legislature of the North West Territories in 1898, to the Alberta Legislature in 1909, and to the House of Commons in 1911. In Edmonton during a railway policy debate, he set a record for oratory with a speech that lasted exactly five hours.

The Conservatives named him national leader in 1927. After his party won the 1930 elections, he served as prime minister for five frustrating years. Defeated in 1935, he moved to England in 1939. He had said he would "live and die in Calgary." But Viscount Bennett of Mickleham, Calgary, and Hopewell died in Surrey. He's buried there.

He was a wealthy man, inheriting in 1921 a large holding in the E. B. Eddy paper companies. His first, instinctive reaction to the depression was to resort to private philanthropy. Individuals who wrote to him might hope to receive a few dollars through the mail.

But he never could win over the poor. With no money for gas or repairs, farmers couldn't run their cars. They took out the motors and pulled the frames with horses. They called the contraptions Bennett Buggies.

Inspired, perhaps, by Franklin Roosevelt, Bennett belatedly changed course and came out with his own New Deal calling for minimum wages, unemployment insurance, hospital and crop insurance. Nobody bought it — not in 1935, though all these things would be adopted after he had been turned out of office.

There was nothing an elected politician in power could do to save himself. In this province, the United Farmers of Alberta experiment also collapsed in 1935. The UFA had been in power in Alberta since 1921.

The guiding genius of the farmers' movement was Henry Wise Wood. It was said that, between 1916 and 1930, he was the most influential man in Alberta. He served as president of both the Alberta Wheat Pool and the UFA. A low-keyed philosopher, he wasn't colorful. His trademark was a straight-stemmed pipe.

His UFA at first wasn't a political party at all. Henry Wise Wood opposed the idea. Gradually, however, the rank and file demanded it, and 1921 saw the first of two incredible political upsets in Alberta. The voters sent to the Legislature 39 successful UFA candidates, 14 Liberals, 4 Labor candidates, 3 Independents, and 1 Conservative.

For 50 years Calgary and Alberta spurned the "old line" political parties. The United Farmers of Alberta philosophy was largely the personal philosophy of H. W. Wood. He could have been premier. But he didn't want the job, and never accepted it.

The UFA was characterized by its lofty moral fervor. Farmers had their special interests. But the UFA farmers saw themselves as both capitalists and laborers, and thus the logical channel through which the deadlock between organized capital and organized labor could be broken. Their movement would evolve into "one co-operative unit in the interest of human welfare" until there was nothing left to exploit except the gifts of Nature herself.

It sounds too good to be true, and in any case the depression and the failings of the UFA government had the 1935 electorate looking desperately for something different. They found it in Social Credit. The voice of William Aberhart was being heard throughout the land.

'Bible Bill' arrives

William Aberhart, as Herald cartoonist Stewart Cameron saw him during the 1930s. The Alberta premier's dreams of controlling the press made him a frequent target in the newspapers.

During the winter of 1970-71, as many as 2,100 fired-up youngsters crammed themselves into a drab brown building at 516 8th Ave. S.W., in downtown Calgary. The attraction was a series of hard-rock concerts organized by CFCN television, which was taping a show called Come Together for the CTV national network. The press of the crowd and the throbbing beat of the bands was such that a less sturdy building might have collapsed under the strain.

Subsequently abandoned and boarded up, the building once served a vastly different purpose. It was the Prophetic Bible Institute, the launching pad from which William Aberhart put Social Credit into orbit over Alberta. That it ever would become a discotheque was inconceivable in the 1930s. The anthem that echoed then through the huge two-storey hall was O God Our Help in Ages Past.

By 1935 Albertans stood at a crossroads. Crushed by the depression, they were ready to try anything that promised a way out. They might have embraced socialism. The groundwork for a new left-leaning political alliance had been laid here in Calgary a few years earlier.

A 1932 meeting in the Legion Hall attracted 1,300 farmers, labor leaders, and socialists from the four western provinces. They passed a resolution, moved by M. J. Coldwell, calling for a new system of socialism and co-operative production. It was the beginning of the Co-Operative Commonwealth Federation (CCF), which formally came into existence in Regina the following year.

One man charted an entirely different course for Alberta. From the pulpit of the Prophetic Bible Institute, William Aberhart preached fundamentalist religion and talked about an untried economic theory that nobody understood. His powers of persuasion were such that the people bought Social Credit without caring that they didn't understand it.

The economic theory never worked, but the Social Credit government of Alberta ruled with a firm and paternalistic hand for 36 years. During those years, visitors to Calgary were understandably perplexed. What, they always, and not unreasonably, wanted to know, is Social Credit? All the natives could do was shrug, smile, and try to change the subject.

The theory of Social Credit first was advanced in England by a Scottish mechanical engineer, Major C. H. Douglas. He talked about how there never was enough money available for people to buy everything that was being manufactured. Reform the system of distribution, he said, and everybody could be happy and prosperous.

The Alberta brand of Social Credit was defined by Aberhart, not Douglas. In 1935, voters were told to forget about the theory. Elect a Social Credit government. The government would hire experts. The experts would work out the details.

Who possibly could buy a pig-in-a-poke like that? Alberta, as it turned out, was more than ready to buy it. Eastern Canada needed food. Alberta had wheat and livestock, and no buyers. Eastern Canada manufactured clothes. Practically nobody here had money to buy clothes or anything else. Obviously, there was something terribly wrong with the economic system.

And, in 1935, there was another, decisive factor in the equation. William Aberhart's stature by then was such that people could accept something like Social Credit simply because he asked them to accept it.

To inspire such allegiance, he had to be an extraordinary man. And he was. There were various opinions about him, pro and con, but nobody ever denied he was formidable. It was possible to dislike him, but nearly impossible to fight him.

He came here from Ontario and became principal of Crescent Heights High School. The school dominated the sparsely-settled North Hill. Meticulous and demanding, Aberhart dominated the school. As a Bible teacher, he was equally zealous. He was tireless, whatever the pursuit and however long the hours.

A most descriptive portrait of this imposing figure can be found in *The Social Credit Movement in Alberta*, a history by John A. Irving.

Aberhart's amazing capacity for work, Irving relates, was made possible by his robust physique and excellent health. He was a man of size and stature, blue-eyed, tall, and heavily built. His followers believed that "his large head, which had only a fringe of hair at the sides and back, was of the shape and type that inevitably houses brains."

A pince-nez added to the general appearance of a man of distinction. The voice was "clear, pleasant, sonorous, and capable of great range and volume, and he learned to manipulate its curious undertones with highly dramatic effect." The voice was not only unique, but also contagious. His successor, Ernest Manning, came to sound exactly like him. On radio they were interchangeable.

Aberhart has been called a fanatic, and worse, but here is John Irving's verdict:

"If he was narrow, he was not ascetic, for he loved good food, good clothes, and good cars. Such concessions to the flesh-pots redeemed him from fanaticism. He had a sense of humor, somewhat primitive, kept in bounds by a sense of decorum."

He was 31 years old when he came here in 1910. He founded the Calgary Prophetic Bible Conference, a men's Bible study group, in 1918. The group eventually claimed 2,200 adherents.

The surge to province-wide prominence came when radio discovered Aberhart, and vice-versa. The historic first broadcast took place in November, 1925. CFCN strung a phone line from its studios to the Palace Theatre. The stage was cluttered with wires and technicians.

Irving describes Aberhart facing the microphones "in abject terror". Later he was to be acclaimed as one of the most effective broadcasters anywhere.

A beaming Aberhart meets his admirers at a Social Credit picnic in 1936 marking the party's first anniversary in power. The event was staged on St. George's Island.

Elect Manning, Irwin, Anderson, Bowlen, Gostick, Hugill

Today's Weather
FORECAST—Cloudy and unsettled.
TEMPERATURE—Calgary, 3 p.m. 47.
August 24—Sunrise 5:55; Sunset 7:42.

THE CALGARY DAILY HERALD

5 O'CLOCK EDITION

FIFTY-SECOND YEAR   CALGARY LOCAL   CALGARY, ALBERTA, FRIDAY, AUGUST 23, 1935   24 PAGES

SOCIAL CREDIT LANDSLIDE

MUCH GRAIN FORECAST TO GRADE LOW

C.N. Survey Indicates Wide Variation In Yield

WEATHER HOLDS UP HARVESTING

Five Bus. to Bumper Crop Prediction For Alberta

(Special Dispatch to the Herald)
WINNIPEG, Aug. 23. — Cool weather with varying amounts of precipitation has interrupted harvesting operations in many districts, according to the weekly report of the Canadian National Railways.

Hail storms with varying amounts of precipitation have also wrought their toll, with frost damage of a weak age is only now becoming apparent.

Crop yields are hard to estimate even in rust-infested districts, some fields of red spring are yielding as high as 15 bushels to the acre while many fields are being left uncut. One thing is certain, the report says the 1935 crop will contain a considerable percentage of low grade samples.

In North and South-Central Manitoba cutting of coarse grains and threshing of wheat was delayed by rain. When the weather clears barley and oat crop will rapidly be completed, and by the end of August a considerable percentage of grain will be in the bins.

Threshing Starts

In North-Central Manitoba, and through the English Swan River districts cool weather with heavy rains brought harvesting to a standstill. About 50 per cent. of cutting has been completed but in some localities threshing has started.

Along the Lenwood, Lampman, Arcona, Gravelbourg Central Butte, Moosebank, borough sub-division of Saskatchewan cutting is general and some threshing has been done.

Damage from rust has been heavy and in some districts little wheat will be threshed, while in others where combines are working, wheat is averaging from 10 to 15 bushel per acre, but grading low.

Threshing of fall rye is about completed and yields have been good. Grasshoppers are still working in some localities and causing considerable damage in late crops.

From Yorkton through the Melville, Wadena, Biggar, Dodsland, Rosetown, Elrose districts the weather has been cooler and a frost was reported last week which damaged garden stuff to some extent but has not caused material damage to grain crops.

Light Frosts

In South-Central Alberta the weather has been cool with scattered showers and some light frosts. Yields in this area will be variable and will produce from about five bushels in some districts to bumper crops in others.

Cutting has commenced in north-central districts of Alberta but it will not be general until some time next week.

Weather has been cool and cloudy and the damage from frost of last week has not yet been determined but where grain was in the milk stage damage will be severe.

Five weather has prevailed in the Peace River district and grain is ripening fast. Frosts have caused slight damage.

C.P.R. Report

Late crops have filled out but vesting operations have been resumed, and a fair percentage of wheat is cut throughout the west, despite variable weather during the last week, says the Canadian Pacific Railways' report.

In Southern Alberta, cutting is general, and is also under way in the east-central portion of the province. Frost hit North-Western Saskatchewan and parts of North-Central and Northern Alberta, causing considerable damage to vegetable and grain crops, estimated from 30 to 75 per cent. damage according to locality, the Killingan subdivision of the railway suffering most.

Since Tuesday fair weather has been favorable to the drying of grain in the north, and moderate to heavy rains in Manitoba, Saskatchewan and South-Western and Central Alberta have helped fill out the late grains.

90 Per Cent. Cut

Manitoba says the crop is estimated 84 per cent. cut and threshing commenced with 91 per cent. of the same time last year; 80 per cent. cut, and 40 per cent of barley in San-...wheat it is estimated 78 per cent. for wheat and Alberta, 50 per cent. for wheat, with coarse grains at 51... and in both of these provinces.

Rust inroads are reported in Central and Northeastern Saskatchewan threshing returns verifying the report of damage to coarse grain.

Alberta's sugar beets are prospering and British Columbia's larger fruits are moving in large volume, and a record of peaches and berries is reported, with general crops progressing to a good yield and pasturage excellent.

NEGRO ELECTROCUTED
TUCKER PRISON FARM, Ark., Aug. 23. — A Negro, named Amanda Crump, shortly negro was electrocuted here today for the murder of his commonlaw wife, Amanda Brown.

New Party Registers Overwhelming Win Provincial Election

Alberta to Have First Social Credit Gov't in World — Cabinet Ministers Go Down to Defeat as U.F.A. Administration Routed; Only Hon. J. F. Lymburn Stands Chance of Retaining Seat.

Opposition May Total Four

FLASH

The standing at 1 p.m. was:

Social Credit elected	38
Liberals elected	2
Conservatives elected	1
Social Credit leading	21
U.F.A. leading	1
Total seats	63

(By Canadian Press)

EDMONTON, Aug. 23.—Alberta will have a Social Credit government, headed by William Aberhart, the 57-year-old Calgary founder of the Alberta Social Credit League.

In its initial bid for power, and the first time the electors of a Canadian province have ever been offered a social credit administration, the league candidates made a sweep of the rural ridings. They were also among the leaders as the proportional representation count proceeded at an early hour this morning in the cities.

Premier Reid, head of the U.F.A. government since 1934, when he succeeded Hon. J. E. Brownlee in the premiership, was defeated by social credit in his riding of Vermilion. He has represented Vermilion in the legislature since 1921, the year the U.F.A. defeated the Liberal regime which had held power from the formation of the province in 1905.

All the Reid cabinet members were defeated, or far behind their opponents, with the exception of Hon. J. F. Lymburn, attorney-general, who was running fifth in the six-seat Edmonton constituency in the second count here.

W. R. Howson, the Liberal leader, was re-elected on the first choice count in Edmonton, while John Irwin, veteran Calgary member, was the only Conservative in the province to be elected at press time.

Hon. J. E. Brownlee, former premier, who was running for re-election in Ponoka, was defeated by his Social Credit opponent, Mrs. W. W. Rogers, one of the leaders in the new movement.

The Social Credit men made a clean sweep in the southern rural constituencies. In the single member ridings of Medicine Hat and Lethbridge Liberal and Labor stalwarts, members of the last legislature lost. In the north, Liberals and the U.F.A. candidates suffered the heavy defeat.

E. C. Manning, chief aide of Mr. Aberhart in sponsoring the new economic plan, headed the Calgary poll.

Mayor Loses at Drumheller

In Drumheller, centre of a coal mining district, P. C. Moyer, independent party leader in the last legislature, was swept out of office by H. Ingrey the Social Credit candidate. Murdoch Clarke, well known Alberta Communist, trailed at his attempt to gain election in Drumheller as did Duncan McDonald, Liberal.

A. L. McPherson, former minister of public works, who represented Little Bow riding in the legislature, was forced out of office. Rev Peter Dawson, the Social Credit nominee, was the victor. The defeated included L. H. Slack, Liberal.

Surrounded by members of the Social Credit League in Calgary, Mr. Aberhart, who was not a candidate, received the election returns at the Prophetic Bible Institute, which he founded in Calgary some years ago. It was here he organized the Social Credit League.

Constituency Figures

LEGEND

U.F.A.—United Farmers of Alberta (Gov't).
C.—Conservative.
L.—Liberal.
S.C.—Alberta Social Credit League.
Lab.—Labor.
Ind.—Independent.
Comm.—Communist.
Ind.-Lib.—Independent Liberal.
Ind.-Lab.—Independent Labor.
S.T.—Single Tax.
C.C.F.—Co-operative Commonwealth Federation.

(Bracketed after constituency name is result last election, figures indicating majority except in Calgary and Edmonton, where figure, indicate elected members' last-count votes.)

CAMROSE
(U.F.A. 1,051)

*C A. Ronning (U.F.A.)		1,027
*C Johnson (L.)		3,419
W. N. Chant (S.C.)		4,317
(S.C. gain from U.F.A.)		

CARDSTON
(U.F.A. 528)

*G. L. Stringham (U.F.A.)		564
G. D. Wight (L.)		480
L. Tanner (S.C.)		2,078
(S.C. gain from U.F.A.)		

COCHRANE
(U.F.A. 171)

*R M. McCool (U.F.A.)		590
J A. Tweddle (C.)		341
Wm. Laut (L.)		420
Wm. King (S.C.)		1,325
(S.C. gain from U.F.A.)		

DRUMHELLER
(Ind. 77)

*P. C. Moyer (Ind.)		715
Duncan McDonald (L.)		341
H. Ingrey (S.C.)		2,146
Murdoch Clarke (Comm.)		216
(S.C. gain from Ind.)		

LETHBRIDGE
(Lab. 360)

O. W. Green (C.)		1,260
E. Barrowman (L.)		1,946
*A. Neadon (Lab.)		1,043
H. E. Wight (S.C.)		3,700
(S.C. gain from Lab.)		

CFAC

536 K.C.   Phone R1088

The Broadcasting Station of
THE CALGARY DAILY HERALD
Operated by
TAYLOR, PEARSON & CARSON
BROADCASTING CO. LTD.

SPECIAL FEATURES
FRIDAY—August 23

1:00 p.m.—Community Carnival.
2:00 p.m.—Spot Cash.
2:30 p.m.—Nit Wit Court, CRC.
3:30 p.m.—Camp, CRC.
4:00 p.m.—From a Rose Garden.
5:00 p.m.—Sinfonietta, CRC.
5:30 p.m.—Songs from the shows.
6:15 p.m.—Salon Capers.
6:30 p.m.—Frisco, CRC.
6:45 p.m.—Radio Club Night.
7:00 p.m.—Concert.
8:00 p.m.—Cafe Franz Josef.
9:00 p.m.—National Clock, CRC.
10:00 p.m.—Dance.

SATURDAY—August 24

9:00 a.m.—Musical Clock, CRC.
5:00 p.m.—Sports.
6:30 p.m.—Country Sports.
7:15 p.m.—The Dance, NBC, CRC.

Reid Likely To Remain in Power Until Sept. 13

EDMONTON, Aug. 23.—The Reid government will remain in office in this province until September 13 at least, it was shown by provincial election officials today.

While defeated at the polls Thursday, the administration will continue to function as certain formalities have to be carried out in the meantime. The Election Act requires that the returning officers shall make their declarations of the results on the tenth day after the election. As this day falls upon a Sunday and as the next day, Monday, is Labor Day and a public holiday these declarations will not be made until Tuesday, Sept. 13.

Rush Empire Defences in East Africa

Report Britain Plans to Speed Reinforcement Of Troops

LONDON, Aug. 23. (A.P.)—Informed quarters said today the Committee for Imperial Defence had approved plans for speeding up the redistribution and reinforcement of military forces at vital points along the Empire's lines of communications.

The committee met at 10 Downing Street with Acting Prime Minister Ramsay MacDonald presiding.

Plans for strengthening the defences of British territory adjacent to Ethiopia and for the reinforcement of all strategic points along the Mediterranean, the Suez Canal and other African areas have been under way quietly for about two months it was learned, and the decision to speed up the program was regarded as precautionary.

Note to France

The meeting primarily was for the purpose of considering in detail the next move regarding Ethiopia, which is likely to be a note to France. On the nature of the French reply will depend the tenor of fresh representations to Italy.

Ramsay MacDonald viewed the overnight development of the dispute with his initiative cabinet in Downing Street before leaving for Lossiemouth, Scotland. Mr. MacDonald is again acting as prime minister following Stanley Baldwin's return to his vacation on the continent.

George Lansbury, leader of the Labor opposition in Parliament, said today the United States "cannot possibly keep out of the next ...

Lansbury voiced a strong plea, Read Britain's stand. But another, warned the peace of the world depended on the League of Nations.

The ready response of Alberta to the Aberhart plan is remarked here as largely a product of the depression and is illustrating the popular tendency to try any new remedy for economic distress, especially to uproot the existing financial structure and on every line of industry.

No federal significance is read into the result. The issue as understood here, was confined to Social Credit, and in Parliament or any of its parties there is no advocate of a plan of that kind as revolutionary as the Aberhart type. Even by the parliamentary advocates of Major Douglas this particular scheme has always been regarded as visionary.

With, the result such as it is, however, and the financial effect impending, the effect it is thought here may be to cause many federal candidates in the provinces to modify the platform of Social Credit while its popularity severable.

Ottawa cannot conceive of the prospective new ministry at Edmonton being able to set up the Utopia, with which the idea of the people of Alberta will have been fired away completely.

Patenaude Created Knight in St. John Of Jerusalem Order

QUEBEC, Aug. 23. (C.P.)—Hon. E. L. Patenaude, lieutenant-governor of Quebec was today created a knight of the order of the Hospital of St. John of Jerusalem by His Excellency the Governor-General, according to announcement from the vice-regal quarters at the citadel.

Lt.-Col. D. B. Papineau, A.D.C. to the lieutenant-governor, was made a serving brother of the order.

The decision awarded Lieut.-Governor Patenaude does not constitute any special rank or title.

New Leader at Home

The above pictures, taken this morning show the home of William Aberhart, Calgary, leader of the victorious social credit forces. Mr. Aberhart lives at 2505 Fifth Street W. The high school principal political leader is depicted below in his garden.
—Photos by Herald Staff Reporter.

CRISIS LOOMS IN BELGRADE

BELGRADE, Aug. 23 (C.P. Havas)—Three members of the Jugoslav cabinet resigned today, threatening to precipitate a general cabinet crisis.

Nicolas Preca, minister of social welfare, Ignaz Stefanovitch, minister of forests, and Lioubevit Auer, minister of justice, announced their resignations. They were the indirect result of formation of the new government, Radical Union Jugoslav party.

Political circles here hoped a general cabinet reorganization could be averted until after the Little Entente conference called for next Thursday at Bled, to discuss policy at Geneva.

Gov't Grants Rail Orders

Five Eastern Plants Will Manufacture $9,821,563 Worth of Equipment

OTTAWA, Aug. 23 (C.P.)—Railway equipment orders amounting to $9,821,563 have been allocated to five manufacturing plants in Eastern Canada, Snaps of the Canadian National Railways will make factory assignment to the value of $1,325,000. Details of the orders under the supplementary Public Works Act of 1935 were made public today.

An appropriation of $15,00,000 was provided in the act for railway purposes. The two railway companies will have the benefit of the equipment for two years without interest after which they will pay off the principal in instalments, with interest at 4 per cent.

Canadian National will secure $6,791,155 worth of new cars and locomotives, and the Canadian Pacific orders will total $4,253,408.

The Canadian Car and Foundry Company of Montreal will get equipment to the value of $8,613,549; the Eastern Car Company, New Glasgow, N.S., $1,886,175; the National Steel Car Company, Hamilton, $2,582,539; Montreal Locomotive Works $1,166,900; and the Canadian Locomotive Works, Kingston, $492,900.

ACCUSE PAIR OF MURDER

CHICAGO, Aug. 23. (A.P.)—Sergt. Bernard Wolf of the Cleveland police homicide squad, today announced the arrest of Miss Helen Hirman, pretty 30-year-old blonde, and Frank Edward Dolezal, 30, both of Chicago, as suspects in the slaying April 11 of Alex Wesoski, Cleveland butcher.

Ottawa Fears Alberta Economy and Industry Endangered By Scheme

(By the Calgary Herald's Ottawa Bureau)
(Copyright Southam Publishing Co. Ltd.)
By CHARLES BISHOP

OTTAWA, Aug. 23.—Political parties at Ottawa scanned this morning the results of the Alberta elections with some degree of awe at the almost unanimous character of the sweep for Social Credit but with more as to the defeat of the U.F.A. government.

For some time advices received here have indicated that the plank of William Aberhart, proclaimed from the Prophetic Bible Institute at Calgary, has caught on with an evangelical fervor. In that condition it was suggested that anything might happen to the older contending parties. The Conservatives appeared to expect defeat. The Liberals had high hopes of winning up to a month or so ago, but these hopes long since began to fade, according to reports here.

4 SOCIAL CREDIT, CONSERVATIVE AND LIBERAL WIN HERE

Record Vote of 41,193 Cast in City Election As E. C. Manning, Chief Lieutenant for Social Credit Leader, Heads Poll

Eliminate Labor Candidates

On the crest of the wave that swept through the length and breadth of the province, Calgary section of the provincial social credit party elected four out of six candidates in the provincial elections held Thursday, one Conservative and one Liberal candidate also were chosen.

The new M.L.A.'s for Calgary are E. C. Manning, Fred Anderson, Mrs. E. G. Gostick and John W. Hugill, K.C. all members of the social credit party; John Irwin, Conservative, and John J. Bowlen, Liberal.

Manning was the only candidate elected on the first count. Irwin, who finished in second place, was elected on the 12th count when he secured a large number of second choice votes from Hugh C. Farthing, K.C., former Conservative M.L.A., who was eliminated. Anderson, Bowlen, Hugill and Gostick were elected on subsequent counts.

The final standing of the six successful candidates was as follows: E. C. Manning, 8,087; Irwin, 6,692; Anderson, 6,639, Bowlen, 8,478, Mrs. Gostick 5,986 and Hugill, 4,399.

Calgary voters marched to the polls Thursday in huge numbers and when the last ballot box was sealed at 7 o'clock in the evening it was found that a new all-time record had been set. No less than 41,193 votes were cast, nearly double the number polled in the 1930 election.

With a quota of 5,880, set, E. C. Manning, aide-de-camp of William Aberhart, Social Credit party leader, was elected on the first count. One of the surprises of the election so far as Calgary was concerned was the utter rout of the Calgary Labor party candidates. All three candidates Alderman F. J. White, W. G. Southern and A. J. Lissemore lost their deposits.

In order that the data of the standing of the six successful candidates be available in full detail, The Herald is publishing the final figures below:

ALBERTA COAL COMMISSIONER ON WAY HERE

LONDON, England, Aug. 23.—Sir Montagu Barlow, former parliamentary secretary to the ministry of labor in the Conservative government, leaves immediately for Alberta to preside over the Royal commission on the Alberta coal industry.

He expects to arrive in Edmonton the first week in September, accompanied by Liddy Barlow, and also W. Armour, senior official of the Coal Mines Reorganization Commission, who will act as expert adviser to the Royal Commission in Alberta.

Moose Jaw Quits Sask. Rugby Union

MOOSE JAW, Sask., Aug. 23 (C.P.)—Protesting against the use of imported American players in Western Canadian rugby football, the Moose Jaw Millers at a meeting of play-ers and executives voted in favor of withdrawing from competition for the 1935 season. The Saskatchewan Rugby Football Union will be informed of the decision at its meeting on Saturday night in Moose Jaw.

B.C. BANDITS BREAK CORDON

LILLOOET, B.C., Aug. 23 (C.P.)—Three bandits who held up the Bank of Toronto at the Pioneer Mine Tuesday and escaped with $11,135 in cash crashed through a police cordon early today and escaped across the Fraser River here after holding up two special constables guarding the bridge.

The Weather
HERE AND ELSEWHERE

Mostly Fair

The weather has been mostly fair, fair today and Saturday; not quite so warm, probably a few scattered thundershowers.

Alberta — Northwest winds; mostly fair today and Saturday; not quite so warm, probably a few scattered thundershowers.

	Max.	Min.
Calgary, clear	67	47
Banff, clear		40
Edmonton, clear		48
Medicine Hat, clear		
Fairview, clear		
Grande Prairie, clear		
Kamloops, clear		
Penticton, clear		
Victoria, fair		
Vancouver, cloudy		
Prince Rupert, rain		
Regina, fair		
Moose Jaw, fair		
Saskatoon, cloudy		
Prince Albert, cloudy		
Battleford, fair		
Swift Current, fair		
Dauphin, fair		
Brandon, cloudy		
Winnipeg, cloudy		
Kenora, clear		
Port Arthur, cloudy		
Toronto, clear		
Ottawa, cloudy		
Montreal, clear		
Quebec, clear		
Halifax		
St. John		
Father Point		
Port Smith		

Southern Dropped

Alderman W. G. Southern was the first candidate eliminated. Of his second choices, Alderman White received 58, Alderman Lissemore received 71, and the remainder were scattered all over the card. The standing remained unchanged. Alderman R. H. Parkyn was eliminated next, and his No. 2 choices...

(Continued on Page Twenty)

SOCIAL CREDIT TOUR PLANNED

Dean Johnson of Canterbury To Aid Organization of Dominion League

TORONTO, Aug. 23. (C.P.)—Very Rev. Hewlett Johnson, D.D., B.Sc., dean of Canterbury, England, will come to Canada in October to aid in organizing a Dominion-wide Social Credit League. It was announced today by E. Burnham Wyllie, chairman of the Douglas Social Credit Association of Toronto.

Wyllie said organization plans would be made as rapidly as possible but that the new body would take no active part in the general election campaign. It was hoped, however, to have candidates available for every constituency by the succeeding election either in five years hence.

The dean, he said, was coming to the Dominion at a request made through Major Douglas, founder of the Social Credit scheme. Prior to his arrival in Canada about the middle of October, Dr. Johnson will make public addresses on the subject in Boston, New York, Philadelphia and Buffalo, which are the more active Social Credit centres.

Itinerary of Dr. Johnson's tour of the Dominion has not yet been completed.

Aberhart broadcasts over CFCN: "he faced microphones in abject terror".

In the mid-'20s, a massive building fund was started. On radio, in letters, pamphlets and newspapers, followers were invited to "buy a brick" for one dollar. All the bricks were in place by October, 1927, and the Prophetic Bible Institute was opened with Aberhart as president and dean.

The Institute was a fortress against "modernism, higher criticism, scepticism, evolution and sectarianism in all its forms." It would bring together and instruct Fundamentalists in the true faith. It would train Sunday School teachers, missionaries, evangelists, singers, and pastors. It would broadcast *the Word of Truth.*

Ernest Manning, hearing the word on the radio at his farm home near Rosetown, Sask., migrated to Calgary and lived for a time in Aberhart's home. He was the Institute's first graduate. His style always was different from Aberhart's, cool and sharp rather than fiery and combative. But he became Aberhart's lieutenant in all his affairs, and he carried on the Social Credit dynasty after Aberhart died in 1943.

Aberhart was slow to embrace both Social Credit and politics. Once he did it was characteristically an all-out, no-holds-barred fight. Over the radio, every Sunday, came exhortations to fight "poverty in the midst of plenty." Social Credit would give everyone $25 a month. That was something everyone could understand.

Enter — and exit — Major Douglas, the founder of Social Credit. He was invited, by a group that had no affiliation with Aberhart, to speak in the Calgary Amories April 27, 1934. Except that popular sentiment demanded it, Aberhart wouldn't even have had a seat on the stage.

When the dust settled, it was Aberhart's night. A dull, plodding speaker, Douglas was a resounding flop. The chant went up, "We want Aberhart."

— 1935 — HERO —

H'RAY FOR ABERHART

HONEST ABE

SWEEPING SOCIAL CREDIT MAJORITY

— 1936-'37 — NERO —

ALBERTA MORALE

ALBERTA BUSINESS

ALBERTA CREDIT

— 1938 — ZERO —

$9100.

TAX PAYER

PROVINCIAL TREASURY BAG

ALBERTA

S.C.

The band played God Save The King. Douglas and Aberhart, according to one account, almost came to blows in a cloak room offstage. Then Douglas went home, leaving Aberhart to take up the torch.

In 1935, having failed to sell its ideas to any of the "old line" parties, Social Credit at last took dead aim at the Alberta Legislature. It still wasn't classified as a political party. It was a "movement."

Social Credit brought to the election campaign tactics that never had been seen before. In radio dramatizations, *"The Man from Mars"* would arrive on Earth, look at the chaos evident everywhere, and wonder why everybody wasn't rushing to embrace the new gospel.

On a summer day, with the temperature close to 100, a crowd of 3,000 brought picnic lunches to St. George's Island and sat for hours listening to Aberhart and seven others. Social Credit picnics, long-winded but meticulously organized, were among the more popular outdoor attractions during the depression years.

The campaign of 1935 contained aspects of a civil war and a religious crusade. The tattered remnants of the UFA were overwhelmed by the eloquence and organizational skills of "Bible Bill" Aberhart. He appealed to the most basic emotions, and his opponents were blasphemous heretics.

Fred Kennedy, then a reporter for The Calgary Herald and later a columnist for The Albertan, covered that ferocious campaign and saw the writing on the walls of the Prophetic Bible Institute. Politicians "of every ilk" began infiltrating the congregation.

"I thought, they're not here to pray," Kennedy recalls. "Then I watched it develop. They began to set up cells (study groups) in private homes. Everybody put a dime in the plate. The movement was financed on dimes. I knew there were cells in every block. Multiply this, and it became a tremendous force."

In fact, there were 63 Social Credit "study groups" in Calgary, 1,600 in Alberta. They made their presence felt on Aug. 22. The result of the 1935 election was Social Credit 56, Liberal 5, Conservatives 2.

Irving describes Aberhart being handed the results at 10:30 p.m., turning pale, and falling against his pulpit. Everybody rose and sang *O God Our Help in Ages Past.*

Cartoonist Cameron gives his version of the Aberhart decline from "hero" to "zero". The sketch was in reference to the $25 dividend which was promised but never delivered. But the premier still had his salary.

E. C. Manning, left standing, at the Prophetic Bible Institute in the early 1940s.

Probably nowhere in the Commonwealth has there ever been such an upset. The previous government, the UFA, elected no one. The new government consisted of 56 MLAs who never had sat in the Legislature before.

Ernest Manning, himself a novice, had to take charge and show the new members around the corridors of power. Aberhart himself wasn't a candidate in 1935. They found a seat for him later.

The morning after the election, some of the faithful lined up at the city hall in Calgary expecting to collect their first $25 dividend. No dividend ever was paid. Every attempt to implement Social Credit ideas, and some of the attempts were half-hearted, was declared ultra vires by the courts of Canada.

A couple of Douglasite advisers came to Edmonton, were mostly ignored, and went home to England. After 1943, Ernest Manning ran a business-like, no-nonsense conservative government. His successor in 1968, Harry Strom, couldn't

hold the fort against Peter Lougheed's bright young Conservatives in 1971.

From 1921, when the UFA ousted the Liberals, to 1971, when the Conservatives defeated Social Credit, it had been 50 years in the political wilderness for the old-line parties.

★ ★ ★

Forty years later, Senator Manning reminisced about the glory years when Social Credit swept everything before it. His uncluttered, medium-small office, in a medium-small office building on Jasper Ave. in Edmonton, was on this day a haven from the storm. Outside it was a dismal Edmonton day, cold, wet, and windy.

Away from the pulpit or podium, with the spotlight turned off, Ernest Manning always was much more relaxed, easy-going and candid. He still is. He confirmed that the story is true about how he bought a radio, picked up an Aberhart broadcast away out there in Saskatchewan, and was instantly converted.

On Aug. 30, 1971, the Social Credit era ended and the Tories took over.

The radio was a $125, three-tube set with goose-neck speaker acquired from the Montgomery-Ward mail order company in Chicago. A summer's wages for threshing paid for it.

It was 15 below on Christmas Eve when Ernest and his brother installed the aerial on their roof. They worked 15 minutes, thawed out, worked 15 minutes more. They were rewarded with recorded music from Saskatoon. They began picking up Aberhart's broadcasts in 1925, and "through that I was brought back to the Christian life."

Young Ernest came to Calgary in January, 1926, when he first met Aberhart. Commuting between the farm and the Bible Institute, he graduated in 1930. The school in those days was open from September to April to accommodate farmers in the off-season. There were night classes year-round for part-time local students.

Radio was new in every respect. From the Institute, "we threw out a signal and it went every which way." There was no commercial broadcasting on Sundays. Taking over what otherwise would have been dead air time, Aberhart and Manning soon had broadcasts on the air Sunday morning, afternoon and evening.

"Stations fell over themselves to get it. It's changed now. You have to fight to get 15 minutes for Christian work."

From 1933 to 1935 Manning drove Aberhart from town to town, selling Social Credit. They had no trouble attracting crowds.

"A public meeting was an event. People got together. We would hold 10 meetings a week, Monday to Friday, then head back to Calgary for the broadcasts. We used curling rinks, skating rinks, often the outdoors. Our favorite was the lumber yard, where people had somewhere to sit down. We had a crude amplifier and a PA system you could hear all over town."

These were the dust-bowl years. Driving at mid-day, motorists kept their headlights on. The new Social Credit party had to hold two organizational conventions, one in Calgary and one in Edmonton, because few had enough money to travel very far.

The election sweep of 1935 remains amazing. Where had the UFA gone? Where was the newborn CCF?

As Mr. Manning explains it, it was simple enough. The UFA's locals had become Social Credit study groups, and Social Credit, not the CCF, had the support of the workers. Particularly militant were the workers at the Ogden Shops. At meetings there, they used the cowcatcher of a big locomotive for a platform.

Closing down the Prophetic Bible Institute didn't end the religious crusade. Its functions are carried on today through a Bible College in northwest Calgary, Bethel Baptist Church in Calgary, and through radio and correspondence schools still supervised by Ernest Manning.

Weadick's grand legacy

The 'Chucks' leave a dusty wake around the track.

Visitors still come to Calgary expecting to find horses in the street. At least once a year, during the Stampede early in July, Calgary tries very hard not to disappoint them. It's become almost a sacred duty. There are many parts of the world where people would never have heard of Canada, let alone Calgary, except for two things: the annual Calgary "rodeo" and the Mounties who always get their man.

Critics contend that the Stampede no longer serves its original purpose, which was to reflect the town's unique frontier heritage. W. O. Mitchell, having lived in High River, which is a lot closer to real cow country than Calgary, argues that "the Stampede's realization of the cattle business is a long way from reality." The chuckwagon races are a great show, "but let's not confuse it with the real thing."

Locally, that's a good way to start an argument. Fred Kennedy, a one-time rodeo rider and former Stampede publicity director, is willing and able to argue the other side.

"The Exhibition and Stampede saved the Western heritage for Calgary," Kennedy declares, "or this would be just another North American city in the rat race for a buck. It gave the kids in the country a desire to stay with their heritage, to ride and rope, and produce their share of champions. Some look down their nose at the Stampede and say it won't last much longer. There are too many sons and grandsons and great grandsons of the Western pioneers still around to ever let that happen."

Senator Harry Hays feels the Stampede makes the city "bigger than life." As long as it's the No. 1 show of its kind — and it still is — it's a unique attraction. And the show should become even better as horses and horse men become rarer. If it's a good show now, it's also becoming an art form.

The Stampede actually always has been more a reminder than a mirror of the frontier days. As early as 1912, when the Stampede started, writers were deploring the disappearance of the real, open-range cowboys. No one can bring them back. If there still are a few of them hiding out in the hills, they prefer to stay there.

The Calgary Exhibition and Stampede isn't a 10-day wonder anyway. It's a 12-month, $9 million-a-year industry catering to everything from hockey and ice shows to circuses and concerts. The Big Four building's chief claim to fame is that in the winter it's the world's largest curling rink.

There was much nostalgia when they tore down the old grandstand in 1973. But there were disgruntled horse players, too, who figured it should have fallen down years earlier. The new grandstand, opened in 1974 and acclaimed as one of the best anywhere, reflects the fact that a big-league operation requires a modern plant. Some of the rustic charm may have been lost, but the Exhibition and Stampede is a big-league operation.

In the beginning it was modest enough. Long before the Stampede was conceived in 1912, the local agricultural society held an annual fair. The first took place in Claxton's Star Rink, on 6th Ave., Oct. 19 and 20, 1886. The tourist trade wasn't much of a factor in 1886, but the whole town turned out to participate.

There were competitions for draft horses, sheep, swine, poultry, home cooking, embroidery, plants and flowers, and prizes for buggies,

carriages and democrats. Horseshoe tossing was among the events for which prizes were awarded. Everything went smoothly and everybody had a good time, until they got around to the baby-judging contest.

Three infants, all boys, were entered, and the proud parents were equally adamant about who the winner should be. The judges, caught in the middle of an impossible situation, tried to resign and slip away, but the parents wouldn't let them. The Herald reported:

The midway at the 1908 Dominion exhibition: a serenity not found on today's midway.

"After some futile attempts to ascertain the weight and age of the exhibits, the judges withdrew to the back of the stage, out of pistol shot range, and came to the conclusion that the only way to avoid bloodshed was to award a prize to each competitor."

As luck would have it, there were no entries in the sheep competition. The prize money set aside for the sheep was hastily requisitioned and shared out among the three babies and their anxious parents. The contest was declared a three-way draw. Everybody went home happy.

The exhibition society, formed in 1884, bought Victoria Park for $235 in 1889, and consequently went broke. The site was away out of town, south along the Elbow, and nobody thought it was worth much. But the city later bought it for the inflated price of $7,000. From then on, the annual exhibition was genuinely a community affair.

The show might have remained a country fair, not much different from similar functions everywhere, except for Guy Weadick, the legendary long, lean cowboy who came here with a Wild West show in 1908 and decided this was the ideal place for something bigger and better.

Weadick was born in Rochester, New York, on Feb. 23, 1885. He and his wife Flores la Due (nee Florence Benson) were among the more colorful riding and roping teams on the vaudeville and rodeo circuits. Weadick was a good rider and roper, but an even better promoter and public relations man.

From the start he had in mind for Calgary the biggest rangeland extravaganza ever held anywhere. He called it the Stampede, a name designed to distinguish it from all the various rodeos, round-ups and frontier days being held elsewhere in Western Canada and the U.S.

The price tag was out of sight, but Weadick persisted, and in 1912 he succeeded in getting the district's "Big Four" ranchers to underwrite the project for $100,000.

The story is that he talked first to George Lane, then to Pat Burns and A. E. Cross. They each agreed to put up $25,000 and added another $25,000 on behalf of Archie McLean, who wasn't present. McLean arrived in town a few days later and said that was fine, it sounded like a good idea.

As it turned out, the $100,000 guarantee wasn't

Guy Weadick, a Stampede legend.

needed. Despite inclement weather, the first Stampede paid its own way and even turned a small profit. The show was acclaimed as "the most colossal and graphic portrayal of pioneer and range existence that has ever been staged in all the world."

Thousands of Indians poured into town and set up tepees, and the "picturesque aborigines" got rave reviews in the local press. Whatever they may have thought about being called picturesque aborigines, an estimated 2,000 of them participated in the first parade.

Guy Weadick, left, and a few of the Stampede 'cowboys' in 1912.

The 1912 Stampede was held Sept. 2-7. Apart from the tepees, an impromptu tent city sprang up across the Elbow to accommodate tourists. Visitors were assured they would be "just as comfortable as in hotels." If they didn't mind rain, mud, and no room service.

Special trains brought visitors and competitors from as far away as Mexico. All the competing cowboys participated in the parade, along with buffalo and ox teams, local pioneers, labor union leaders, and original members of the North West Mounted Police.

Royalty was represented by the Duke of Connaught, governor-general of Canada, and Princess Patricia. In their honor the city erected an incredible arch across Centre St. It was a minor Arc de Triomphe. In large lettering it bore the salutation: *"God Save the King. Calgary welcomes their royal highnesses."*

Less desirable guests also may have been present. "The underground" sent word that dangerous crooks — talented pick-pockets and confidence men — were coming to the Stampede. "Half a dozen of the most astute sleuths in the employ of the Pinkerton Detective Bureau" were hired to discourage them.

The first competitors were mostly working cowboys. The best were mostly Americans. But the hero of the whole affair was indisputably Canadian. He was Tom Three Persons, a young Indian cowboy from the Macleod district. He had been in jail in Calgary for some unspecified reason, but he was out again in time to participate in the Stampede and try to ride Cyclone.

In 1912, Cyclone was the best bucking horse in the world. He had unseated 129 would-be riders. Then Tom Three Persons jumped aboard, rode him to a standstill, and won the riding championship of the world.

With the boots reversed in the stirrups, Guy Weadick's horse leads the funeral procession at High River in 1953.

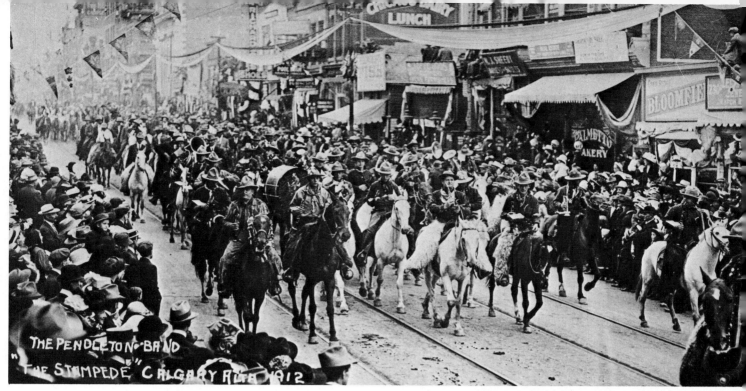

A band mingles with the cowboys during the first Stampede parade.

1912 — the year it all started

Building tops provided an excellent vantage point to view the 1912 parade, right, while at night the Welcome Arch on Centre street, left, dazzled Stampede visitors.

Blood and North Peigan Indians journey into Calgary for the 1912 show.

While the Indians decorated their tepees on the Stampede grounds, Tom Three Persons, left, draws an admiring glance from a youngster.

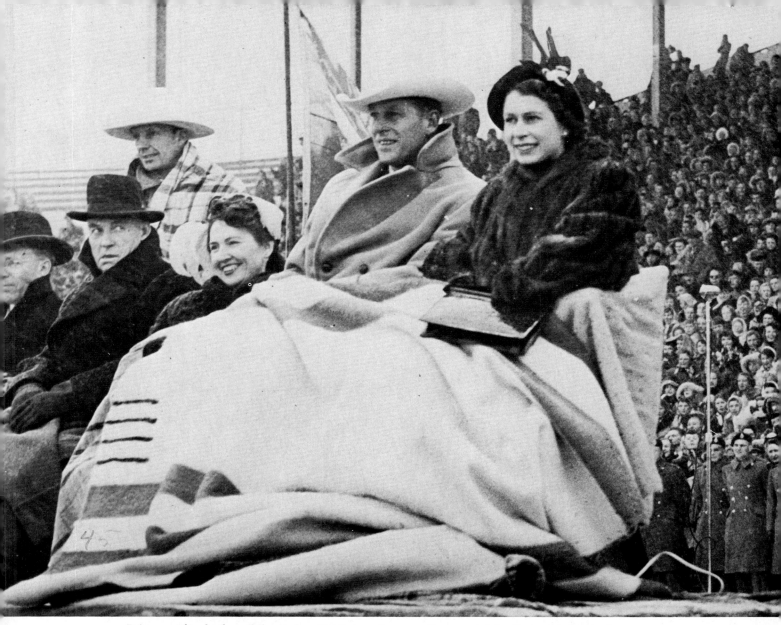

Princess Elizabeth and the Duke of Edinburgh are well wrapped for the special 1951 show.

The second Stampede was a post-war show in 1919, and in 1923 it became the annual Exhibition and Stampede. Guy Weadick managed the rodeo section until 1932. He bought the Stampede Ranch, a dude ranch west of High River where guests could ride, hike, fish or whatever, in 1920, and lived there for many years. He died in California in 1953, and he was buried at High River.

Any list of Stampede rodeo stars over the years would go on almost forever. There was Pete Knight, world's champion bronc rider four times in five years between 1932 and 1936. There was Dick Cosgrave, 10-time chuckwagon champion and the show's most colorful arena director. And there have been dozens of others.

Perhaps a special place in history should be reserved for those hardy cowboys who participated in a command performance for Princess Elizabeth and the Duke of Edinburgh on Oct. 18, 1951, a time of the year ill suited to that kind of outdoor performance.

Victoria Park was frozen solid. A full-scale blizzard whipped 16,000 spectators in the grandstand. Wrapped in electric blankets, the royal couple grinned and enjoyed it. They saw a scaled-down version of the complete show including the chuckwagon races. Riders who fell to the hard-frozen turf that day likely still have bumps and scars as mementos.

In recent years the show-business nature of the Stampede has been underlined by guests such as Walt Disney, Bing Crosby, Bob Hope, Arthur Godfrey, Gracie Fields, Jack Oakie, Burl Ives, Nancy

Greene, Maurice Richard, Bobby Orr, Gordie Howe, and others prominent in entertainment and sports.

The Indians still can make their presence known. Rain marred the 1959 Stampede, and the Stampede Board in its wisdom cancelled all Indian passes except for those living in the Indian village. The Stoneys protested and held a rain dance. Rain sloshed down for three more days. The cancelled passes were restored. The rain stopped, and the sun came out.

Through the 1960s, the Stampede brought in movie and television headliners from Hollywood. Some of the names and their shows have almost faded from memory now, but the list included John Russell (The Lawman), Peter Breck (The Big Valley), Peter Brown (Laredo), Gene Barry (Bat Masterson), Duncan Renaldo (The Cisco Kid), Leo Carillo (Pancho), Rex Allen (various shows), Jay Silverheels (Tonto) and James Drury (The Virginian).

Any resemblance between this lot and the old-time, open-range cowboy was purely illusory. But most of them performed well, particularly in their primary function of keeping the youngsters happy.

Perhaps inevitably, a few performances left something to be desired. Bat Masterson couldn't stand kids, which didn't help, and he wound up making himself thoroughly unpopular. It was reported that a youngster seeking an autograph got Bat Masterson's cane through his toy drum instead. And the Virginian got into a fight with a for-real cowboy, thereby losing half a head of hair and all of his dignity.

But they weren't all losers. The Lawman, Cisco, Pancho and Tonto are fondly remembered. They got into the spirit of the affair and won themselves a lot of new fans. Rex Allen still is a travelling salesman for the Stampede wherever he goes in the U.S.

The story is told about how Peter Brown, learning that a fan of his, a sick child in Frank, Alta., 100 miles away, watched his show every week but couldn't come to Calgary to see him, offered to hop into a car and go to Frank. Someone reminded him that he was due at a high-society barbecue. "Man," he said, "you sure got a lousy sense of priorities." He skipped the barbecue and went to see the youngster.

The Big Four backed the Stampede because they felt their industry, the story of cattle, cowboys and ranchers, shouldn't slip away unremembered. They hardly had in mind a lot of Hollywood cowboys. But it's safe to assume they would have approved of Peter Brown.

They hardly visualized a grandstand show like the Stampede offers now, either, but again they might have endorsed it.

For years it wasn't much of a show The Stampede got what everyone else got, a second-rate touring company playing to the lowest common denominator. Then a Chicago entrepreneur Randolph Avery, came here and organized the Young Canadians. They took over the show and now they're celebrities in their own right, with apologies to no one.

Singers and dancers, professional rodeo stars who compete for big money like touring golf pros, Flare Square, the midway, curling in the Big Four Building, hockey, the Ice Capades and the Shrine Circus in the Stampede Corral, wrestling in the Pavilion — put it all together and, no, it hardly adds up any more to an accurate reflection of the old town as it once was.

Perhaps it isn't even something that could only have happened here. But the fact is it did happen here, its roots go back a long way, and, with its variety of interests, it's a big chunk of Calgary today.

on the next four pages, a Stampede picture portfolio

A group of cowboys at the 1919 Stampede pause between rides for a cool one.

J. M. "Jack" Dillon was for more than 20 years the arena director at the Stampede. Dick Cosgrave, right, was a chuckwagon champion before he became an arena director.

Pete Knight rides Midnight. Below, in 1927 photo.

Tourists line up for free flapjacks and bacon served from a sidewalk stove during Stampede week downtown celebrations.

A rig strikes a barrel and driver Daryl Glen is hurled from the box during
the 1957 Stampede. Glen escaped serious injury.

The new $14.5 million grandstand and race track seats
17,240 people, including 2,700 in the clubhouse on the
second tier.

Chasing the cup

The 1948 Stampeders returned home with the Grey Cup.

One of the goofier Grey Cup football finals on record was played on rain-soaked artificial turf at Vancouver's Empire Stadium Nov. 28, 1971, when the Calgary Stampeders — after a last minute interception, a fumble, an out-of-bounds kick, and a fight — emerged 14-11 winners over the Toronto Argonauts. A classic it was not, but it brought the Grey Cup back to the foothills for the first time in 23 years.

A Calgary team first won the coveted mug in 1948, and that was the year everybody remembers. Calgary defeated Ottawa, 12-7. But what really mattered was the way in which home-town boosters accompanied their team to Toronto and, in their uninhibited fashion, converted an event that was getting to be a bit of a shrug into a national festival.

Since 1948, Calgary always has taken credit for making the Canadian professional football final into the extravaganza it is today. A unique chance to find out if the magic still works looms in 1975. For the first time ever, the Grey Cup game will be played here as part of the city's 100th birthday party.

Lest it be thought that the Grey Cup fun and games are the only thing the city has contributed to the wonderful world of sports, however, a long list

of other achievements should be noted. Calgarians individually, and Calgary teams, have had their moments on the playing fields, and not only in football.

It's recorded that in 1884 soccer, badminton, lacrosse, rugby and tennis were being played on what's now 6th Ave. Polo was popular, reflecting the abundance here of (1) Englishmen and (2) horses. The polo grounds were in Elbow Park, which also boasted a twin race track.

That horse racing would be popular here from the earliest times was only natural. All it required

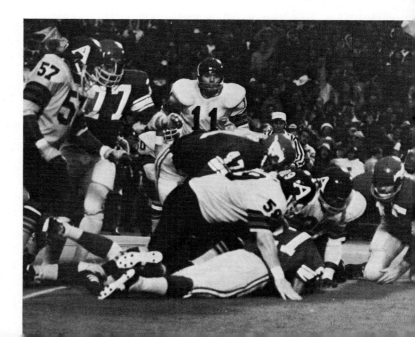

A Toronto Argonauts player fumbles the ball in the dying minutes of the 1971 Grey Cup game. Calgary gets the ball, and the game.

The Calgary Tigers battle the Edmonton Eskimos at Riley Park in October of 1912.

was two riders, two horses, and a bet on who could get from Point A to Point B the fastest. Races were held at Victoria Park long before the first Stampede in 1912. The old half-mile "bull ring" at Victoria Park (now Stampede Park) survived until 1973, when it was replaced by the new, $14 million grandstand and race track complex.

Some of the world's best jockeys started their careers riding on Calgary tracks.

Bill "Smokey" Saunders, who won the U.S. triple crown — the Kentucky Derby, Preakness and Belmont — on a horse called Omaha, grew up in Calgary and learned his trade here. Johnny Longden, who left the coal mines at Taber to ride here as an apprentice, went on to win the triple crown aboard Count Fleet and to set a world record for total wins.

George Woolf, of Cardston, began his career here about the same time as Longden. Many considered Woolf to be the best stakes rider of all time. He twice led the North American jockey standings before being killed in a spill at Santa Anita, Calif., in 1946.

Professional baseball was played at Victoria Park as early as 1907, and an enthusiastic amateur league operated here two years before that.

Among the top amateur teams were The Bartenders, The Barbers, and The Fire Department. They played on Sundays until, one Sunday, as a funeral procession passed by the park, a batter swatted a fast ball through the plate-glass window of a hearse. City Council then passed a bylaw prohibiting Sunday ball.

Capt. A. H. Ferguson, for many years director of high school athletics, is credited with introducing fastball — or softball — in 1908. The game, which also was played indoors in the YMCA and church gymnasiums, was ideally suited to the schools because the grounds were too small for regulation baseball. In 1908, it was a novelty.

Soccer was played on the Athletic Grounds on 12th Ave. E., about where Victoria School now stands. Encouraged particularly by emigrant Englishmen and Scots, it was for a time the most popular sport. Touring teams from overseas came here frequently during the 1920s, attracting crowds estimated as high as 8,000 to 9,000.

The Bowness golf clubhouse, nine miles west of the city, was built in 1912.

176

A polo outing in 1894: later on they moved to Elbow Park.

The Calgary Caledonians, soccer champions of Canada in 1908.

Victoria arena in the 1930s: face-off circle in front of the net.

Calgary's Jamie Paulson became Canada's outstanding badminton player, winning a gold medal in the 1970 Commonwealth Games and a silver medal in the 1974 Commonwealth Games.

A Calgary curling group posed in the 1890s. Col. James Walker is fourth from left, centre row.

One of the more memorable soccer clashes involved the fire department's irrepressible "Cappie" Smart and the police department's individualistic Tom English. Some years later, in 1920, the police department published this account:

"An exciting football game was in progress between the Fire Brigade and a team organized by Chief English. Cappie Smart somewhat damaged one of the opposing players in the game, whereat the Chief commenced waving his famous 'shillelagh' around his head and promising Cappie a sudden and violent death, if he could get at him. Of course, the peppery little Fire Chief invited him to 'get on with it,' and for a few minutes it looked as though there would be a historic fistic exhibition. However, the efforts of the crowd, together with the inherent good sense of the two would-be combatants, prevented any bloodshed."

Tommy Burns, the only Canadian ever to win the world heavyweight boxing title, reigned from 1906 to 1908, moved to Calgary in 1910, and bought a successful clothing business. Since boxing wasn't allowed in the city, Burns went outside the city, as it then was defined, and built an arena in Manchester.

The most celebrated boxing match ever held here ended in tragedy. The combatants were Luther McCarty, the world's white (color was duly noted in those days) heavyweight champion, and one Arthur Pelkey. Burns was in Pelkey's corner when he took on McCarty in the Manchester arena May 24, 1913.

In the first round Pelkey landed a light punch. McCarty fell to the canvas. He was dead. Death

A poster advertised the big match.

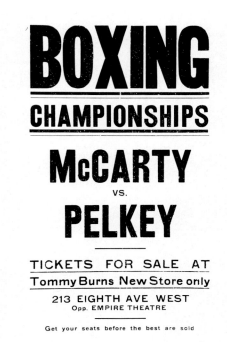

BOXING
CHAMPIONSHIPS
McCARTY
vs.
PELKEY

TICKETS FOR SALE AT
Tommy Burns New Store only

213 EIGHTH AVE WEST
Opp. EMPIRE THEATRE

Get your seats before the best are sold

later was attributed to a riding accident two days earlier. But public opinion of the day was against professional fighting, and Pelkey was brought to trial. With no valid charges against him, he was acquitted.

Serious golfing started in Calgary around the turn of the century. The first "country club" was a little shack west of the Elbow River beside the old General Hospital. Access was via a meandering lane from the city to what's now about 17th Ave. and 6th St. S.E.

A history of golf was written for The Calgary Herald in 1930 by Gordon MacWilliams, city amateur champion in 1926, 1927, 1929 and 1930. He called Calgary in 1930 "the golfiest city in Canada," with more duffers in ratio to population than any other city.

The Bowness Golf Club, nine miles west of the city, was a spectacularly ambitious undertaking in 1912. The clubhouse was a work of art. But it was so far out — "virtually inaccessible" — that to play a round there required "making a day of it."

Tired business men took to the hills around Earl Grey School to practise their shots, and that's how the Earl Grey golf course got started. In 1930, the Calgary Golf and Country Club was cited as the only course in the city with grass greens.

In more recent years, three names have dominated the local golf scene: Keith Alexander, Doug Silverberg and Bob Wylie. Among them, over two decades, they have won the city amateur

championship a total of 15 times, the Alberta amateur 13 times, and the Alberta Open four times. Beyond that, they have regularly represented the province in national competitions and occasionally the country in international competitions.

During the World Amateur in Rome in 1964, Alexander, standing in a sand trap on the 13th hole, saw that Canada could tie for the championship

The Calgary Tigers, hockey champions of Western Canada in 1924-25 season.

Keith Alexander after Calgary match.

Ron Northcott, a titled curler.

Red Dutton and old New York Americans uniform which he put on display in hockey hall of fame.

if he could only break par on four of the last five holes. "It set me up with a feeling of a trance," he recalled later, "and I really wanted to play."

And play he did. He salvaged par on the 13th, sank one-under-par birdie putts on the 14th through the 17th holes, then hit a heel mark and sand trap on the 18th and had to settle for one over par — but it was the kind of late charge Arnold Palmer might envy.

Mention curling, and the name is Ron Northcott. His record: 10 southern Alberta championship titles, six Alberta titles, and the Canadian Brier and World championships in 1966, 1968 and 1969. The late Howard Palmer won the Canadian Brier in 1941. He was the only other Calgarian to do it.

The first hockey game on record here was played in 1888, with 10 players to a side. Some had hockey sticks, the rest used brooms. The puck was a wooden block. They played for 90 minutes on the Elbow River.

Frank Claxton's ice rink at 6th Ave. and Centre St. was the best (and only) covered skating rink in town until it was torn down to make way for Hull's Opera House. The Sherman Rink, at 17th Ave. and 1st St. S.E., was a roller rink or ice rink, depending on the weather. The building catered to social events of all kinds. It was a considerable loss when, at noon, Feb. 25, 1915, the Sherman Rink burned down.

Before it was replaced by the Stampede Corral, Victoria Arena was from 1911 until 1961 "the heart and centre of sporting life in Calgary." Former fire chief Barney Lemieux viewed it dimly as "the biggest potential fire hazard in the city," but that didn't stop the crowds from packing the place. Over the years the cow town has been a great hockey town too.

In 1924 a Calgary team, the Tigers, challenged for the Stanley Cup, no less. Representing the Western Canada Hockey League, they were beaten in the best of three series, 6-1 and 3-0, by the Montreal Canadiens, representing the National Hockey League.

Calgary has helped stock the NHL with some of its best and most colorful players. Among them were Tiny Thompson, Norm Gainor, Herb Gardiner, Red Dutton, Lorne Carr, Sweeney Schriner, Frank McCool, Pat Egan — and the list goes on. The picture gallery in the Corral concourse is a miniature hall of fame.

Among all the names, in whatever sport, Calgary's all-time Sportsman for all seasons would always be Lloyd Turner.

Lloyd came here from Elmvale, Ont., in 1910 as a catcher for a touring baseball team. He stayed here, and in turn managed the Sherman Rink, Victoria Arena and the Corral, retiring in 1964 after a lifetime of dedication to sports. "Day in and day out for 50 years," Leishman McNeill recorded, "Lloyd Turner did more to promote sport in this city than any other individual."

He took over management of the Stampeders, a lack-lustre senior hockey team, in 1945. The following year, under coach Al Arbour, they won the Allan Cup, the hotly-contested senior amateur Canadian title. The final game was played in Edmonton, where the Stampeders beat Hamilton 1-0.

At that time there were no fast airline flights home. The team celebrated in Edmonton and came home aboard an overnight train. Just about the

A special train, loaded with Stampeder fans, got a rousing send-off when it left Calgary in November, 1948.

1948 — how the East was won

Calgary fans took over Toronto's Union Station on arrival for a square dance.

Stampeder supporters let their horses loose in "hog town" and the Ontario city never forgot it.

Calgarians turned out in the thousands to welcome home the 1948 Grey Cup champs.

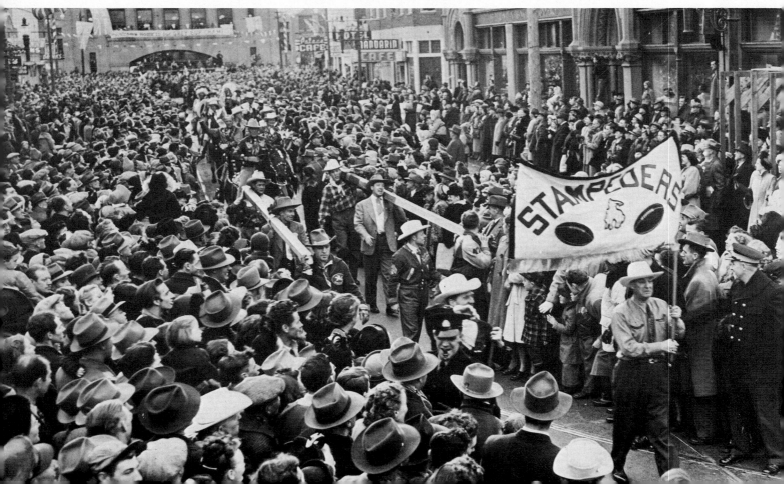

whole town was waiting, and there was a spontaneous parade through the streets. Along with the Grey Cup in 1948, the Allan Cup victory in 1946 ranks among Calgary's finest moments in sports.

Toronto didn't know what to expect in 1948 when the Western champion Calgary football team headed east for the Grey Cup game. Word was that the team and 300 red-eyed supporters were aboard a 13-car special train packed with square dancers, wild cowboys and Indians, and heaven knew what else.

They were aiming to invade the venerable Royal York Hotel. Mayor-to-be Don Mackay, cast in the role of civic goodwill ambassador, recalled that "the Royal York was in a flap. They took every stick of furniture off the main floor. They were petrified."

But Harry McConachie, the chairman in charge of arrangements, working with Mackay, Stu Adams, Ed O'Connor, Bill Herron, Cliff Cross and a dozen other Calgary boosters, had something more in mind than just a big drunk. As the train rolled eastward, they organized a show that Toronto would neither forget nor regret.

Jac Friedenberg, pianist and music teacher, was on board with a four-piece band. They had a piano strapped down in the baggage car. Along the way they used the baggage car to practise square dancing. At each stop everybody piled out onto the

McMahon Stadium under construction. It was finished in 103 working days.

platform for an impromptu show. By the time they reached Toronto, they were a well-drilled aggregation.

"When we got into the Royal York," Don Mackay recalled, "we started square dancing. We

Another Grey Cup celebration, this one in Vancouver in 1971.

had prearranged for each guy to pick a girl and each girl to pick a guy out of the crowd. We rocked that hotel, but it was a high-level effort."

Friedenberg remembers the hotel's guests standing along the balcony in the lobby in a state approaching abject terror. He was perturbed to find the hotel had its piano padlocked. The management, faced with this wild horde, wasn't taking any chances at all.

The upshot wasn't the riot that everybody apparently feared. The Calgarians won over their hosts with dancing, chuckwagons and free flapjacks. Cowboys and Indians, horses and wagons enlivened the Grey Cup parade as never before. Toronto's Mayor Hiram B. MacCallum wound up riding in the parade in a western outfit. The Royal York wound up inviting everybody back.

The team returned in 1949, but lost, and it was a long time between Grey Cups after that. Regardless, the 1948 crowd accomplished something lasting. Before 1948, the Grey Cup wasn't a national festival. After 1948, it was. And 1975, with the game being played here, affords an opportunity to rejuvenate it all over again.

In 1960, the manner in which Calgary acquired what sports columnist Jim Coleman has called "Canada's finest football facility" was a typical Calgary undertaking. Oil men George and Frank McMahon decided this place needed something better than old Mewata Park. They put up $300,000 to get the job started and underwrote another $400,000 to finish it.

The main contract went to Burns and Dutton Concrete and Construction Co. Ltd. The company president was flamboyant Mervyn "Red" Dutton, legendary pro hockey star in Calgary, Montreal (the Maroons) and New York (the Americans) and a former president (1944-45) of the National Hockey League.

These high-powered tycoons wanted their ball park ready for the 1960 football season. Starting in the spring, contractors and sub-contractors finished the project in 103 working days. Every existing speed record for a job of this magnitude, a 21,000-seat stadium with natural grass rated superior to artificial turf, fell by the wayside.

At an inaugural luncheon in the Palliser Hotel, Dutton handed 1,500 one-dollar bills to George McMahon. He had bet that the stadium couldn't be finished that fast. Appropriately, after the dust had settled, they named the place McMahon Stadium.

The Stampeders don't always "go", but the fans never give up.

The gamble pays off

Dingman No. 1 in the Turner Valley.

During the fourth quarter of its first century, the town changed almost beyond either recognition or redemption. It was almost as if someone had taken the old town and slapped a new city on top of it, letting the spillover wash up the hills and out across the plains. The reason, in a word, was oil.

The rest of the country always has tended to view this part of the country in a simplistic sort of way. The average Calgarian was a cowboy riding on a horse. Overnight, the cowboy became wealthy. Trying to keep pace with the image hasn't been easy. Calgarians have to work harder to remember who they really are.

The metamorphosis from cow town to oil town began with the historic Imperial Oil discovery up north near Leduc in February, 1947. What followed wasn't the town's first oil boom — they had been occurring off and on since the turn of the century — but it was the biggest. Thanks to the earlier discoveries, Calgary was able to cash in on the big one. The place never has been the same since Leduc, nor will it ever be.

The search for oil in these parts dates back to well before the turn of the century. Allan P. Patrick, a topographical surveyor from Ottawa, filed an oil claim at Waterton Aug. 26, 1889. He was so far ahead of his time that the government didn't have an appropriate application form to give him. Instead he was registered as the discoverer of a quartz mine, with quartz stroked out and petroleum written in.

Carl O. Nickle, who began publishing his Daily Oil Bulletin 10 years before Leduc, traces the story of oil in southern Alberta back to a couple of characters improbably called Lafayette French and Kootenai Brown.

For generations the Indians had been skimming a brown, oily liquid off the surface of a foul-smelling slough in ranching country near Pincher Creek. Recognizing it as crude oil Kootenai and Lafayette sought to buy the slough. There was

Workers at the Dingman well in 1914 fill a barrel with oil.

much haggling. Finally, the Indians surrendered their rights to the slough for a horse.

Though the automobile hadn't been invented, crude oil served various functions. It could be used, for example, as axle grease. And the medicinal value of petroleum was well known. In particular, it was highly regarded as a laxative.

A place called Oil City, 25 miles southwest of Pincher Creek and five miles north of the U.S. border, came into existence in 1899. It wasn't a city — just a few shacks — and there wasn't much oil to be found, but the name attracted interest.

A group of Calgarians formed the Rocky Mountain Development Company in 1901. The group included A. P. Patrick, John Lineham, George Leeson and Arthur Sifton. The latter later became premier of Alberta. But the company never found the source of the Waterton oil seepages, and the first oil boom sputtered out.

The first "oil men" weren't really oil men at all. They were farmers, ranchers, business men, or whatever. They knew more about real estate and when they did find oil they sold it like real estate.

It was natural, therefore, that when oil was discovered in significant quantities at Turner Valley in 1914, the fast-fading land boom of 1912-13 was converted immediately into an oil boom. Calgary was caught up in a new wave of excitement that lasted about three months. Then, in August, 1914, the First World War snuffed it out along with everything else.

Turner Valley always had been great farming and ranching country. People noticed, however, how the place didn't smell good. Sulphurous gas oozed up here, there, and everywhere through cracks and fissures in peculiar rock formations studding the land.

The smelly stuff acquired new significance with the advent of the horseless carriage. Now everyone was looking for this wonderful fluid that made the cars run.

William Stewart Herron, who owned a ranch, hauled coal, and ran a boarding house near

A. W. Dingman, holding pipe, watches his black gold pour out before visitors in July, 1914.

Okotoks, became Turner Valley's first big oil promoter. One day in 1911, the story goes, he brought a small group of men to his ranch. To convince them he had something, he put a match to a fissure of escaping gas, then fried bacon and eggs in a pan over the evenly-burning flame.

The visitors were impressed. William Elder and A. W. Dingman pooled their resources with W. S. Herron, formed the Calgary Petroleum Products Company, and drilled the well that went into the books as the Dingman discovery. Dingman was the expert who knew how to go about drilling a well. The others knew how to promote it.

The discovery well blew in, in May, 1914, at a depth of 2,718 feet, with a flow of about 4 million cubic feet daily of wet gas saturated with straw-colored oil. The real oil pool was farther down, but at the time no one cared. The light-gravity naphtha (natural gasoline) was so pure that the backers of the discovery well — so the story goes — poured it straight into their automobiles and drove back to Calgary to spread the good news.

Carl Nickle has recorded what happened then:

"The boom that followed is historic. Ordinary business in Calgary came to a standstill. Hundreds of brokerage houses sprang up all over the city. Literally hundreds of companies were formed and, with practically every person with a dollar in his pocket striving to get in on the ground floor, as much as $500,000 changed hands daily.

"Three months later the boom collapsed, largely because of the outbreak of the First World War."

Imperial Oil got into the act in 1921 through a subsidiary, Royalite Oil Company, that took over the Dingman discovery. In October, 1924, Royalite No. 4 drilled into hard limestone at 3,740 feet, stopped, then blew in with 21 million cubic feet per day of gas accompanied by 500 barrels a day of high-gravity naphtha.

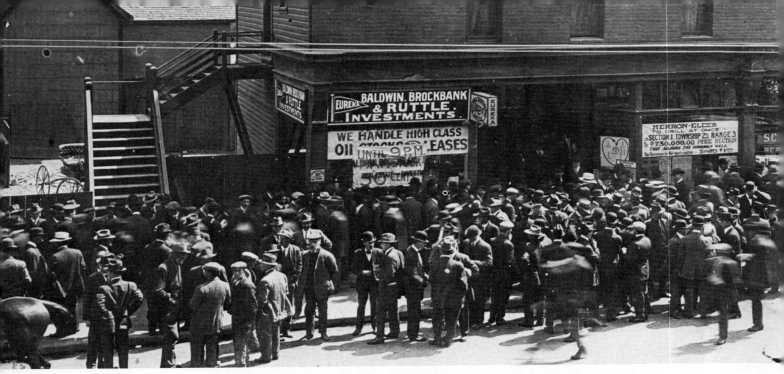

Eager investors wait for a chance to buy more oil stocks in 1914.

Signs of the times: the oil boom of 1914 sparked a stock bonanza that
brought ordinary business in Calgary to a standstill. The scene
here is the old Windsor Hotel on Centre Street.

The well blew wild, and for years to come that corner of Turner Valley was known as Hell's Half Acre. To get the oil out, they flared millions of cubic feet of waste gas. Turner Valley was a bright glow in the sky southwest of Calgary every night. It attracted speculators like moths.

The Turner Valley madness affected almost everyone in Calgary. Housewives invested their housekeeping money. It's said anyone could buy oil stocks, along with railway tickets, through the ticket wicket at the CPR station.

Oil stocks were auctioned off. The auction rooms were so busy they kept their money in wastepaper baskets. When the auction rooms closed, no one wanted to go home. Curbside brokers took over, everybody trying to hustle everybody else. Fred Kennedy, who came here with his family in 1912, remembers selling stock out of a newsboy's bag in front of the Palliser Hotel.

Stocks worth 5 or 10 cents in the morning might be trading for $1 by nightfall, then collapse just as quickly. Carl Nickle relates how one U.S. promoter tried to "salt" a Turner Valley well. He poured in a barrel of oil at night, then bailed it out for the edification of would-be speculators the next morning.

There weren't many rules, but this fellow went too far. He was one of the few who wound up in jail.

Calgary in the 1920s had a reputation as the "most speculative" town in Western Canada. Offices were vacated, and it seemed no one was working. The brightly-lit night sky to the southwest was a constant distraction during the week. On Sundays, to see for themselves what was going on, many would undertake the long, arduous drive down the dirt road from Calgary to Turner Valley.

Carl Nickle sees it as another manifestation of the gambling spirit that brought the Mounties, railway builders and settlers to the frontier. The climate was favorable for gamblers of all kinds.

The losers were those who bought stock that inevitably was worthless. Some of the craftier promoters had the thing rigged so they couldn't lose. They assigned stock to themselves, paid themselves a commission for selling it, and paid themselves a salary. Oil or no oil, they had it coming and going.

When Turner Valley Royalties No. 1 blew in it swept Alberta into the oil world once and for all. The year was 1936.

Calgary oilmen, left to right, Sam Nickle, Carl Nickle, Eric Harvie and Max Bell.

J. Grant Spratt, an independent petroleum consultant who came here in 1926 as a geologist for the federal government, figures the promoters still needed "terrific nerve." The fact is nobody, promoter or investor, knew what he was getting into. In 1926, Grant Spratt was one of the very few qualified geologists around.

Ten years later, one well, Turner Valley Royalties No. 1, established the Turner Valley field once and for all. The Royalties well proved an old theory that crude oil could be found by drilling still deeper, beyond the gas and naphtha formations.

The timing couldn't have been better. In 1936, the West was stagnating in the depths of the depression. The Royalties discovery didn't turn it all around overnight, but it helped. It was the first piece of good news the deflated economy had received since 1929.

The Royalties well was launched in 1934 when the late Robert A. Brown, then superintendent of the Calgary Street Railway system, and the late George M. Bell obtained a 60-acre lease. Turner Valley Royalties was incorporated. George Bell died in March, 1936, and his son Max replaced him on the board of directors.

The method of financing was unique. No one had any faith left in common stocks, legitimate or otherwise. Instead of shares, Brown and Bell sold royalty interests. For $1,500, an investor owned 1 per cent of the well. Money still was short, and the Royalties team needed a $30,000 loan from the British American Oil Company to complete its discovery.

After the Royalties strike, Major James R. Lowery's Home-Millarville No. 2 became the most prolific oil well in the British Empire. Major Lowery was a former Edmonton lawyer. His No. 1 well at Millarville was a failure. He drilled 6,000 feet down — and across. The pipe at the bottom veered 2,000 feet away from the wellhead at the top.

Hit-and-miss drilling like that still was common in the 1930s. But Millarville No. 2, drilled straight down, more than compensated for No. 1. The record-breaking well pumped 2 million barrels of oil.

The flaring of gas continued into the 1930s. Pilots flying in here used it as a beacon. The regulatory agencies that finally put both the boiler-room stockbrokers and the free-flowing gas wells under control came into existence during the '30s.

During the Second World War, the Turner Valley field enabled the prairie provinces to be self-sufficient in oil. After the war, oil companies poured $50 million into exploration and development in Western Canada. They found only a few small gas fields and some heavy crude in a small field at Lloydminster.

Many of the major exploration companies had given it up as a bad job when, on Feb. 13, 1947, the

"It's oil, oil," shouted a driller at the wellhead. And indeed it was. On Feb. 13, 1947, near Leduc, Imperial Oil struck it big. In this photo a crowd gathers around the drilling rig that first day.

Imperial-Leduc discovery near Edmonton turned it all around once and for all.

Thanks to Turner Valley, Calgary was well situated to cash in on the post-1947 boom. The oil was near Edmonton, but the Oil and Gas Conservation Board, the oil lawyers and other experts, and the old Turner Valley companies all were situated here.

And U.S. oil men, rushing back to cash in on the Leduc discovery, found that the airline connections weren't all that good. If they were coming up from the south, they could fly only to Great Falls. They would rent a car there and drive north. The first "oil capital" they hit was Calgary.

Thus Calgary became the headquarters and administration centre for the oil industry in all of Canada. If it had gone to Edmonton instead, Carl Nickle believes, Calgary today would be a small, struggling, backward place. Edmonton, with oil in addition to the provincial capital, the university and everything else, would have left this town hopelessly behind.

There have been a lot of rags-to-riches stories along the way. And a lot of riches-to-rags stories. During the lean years, some oil millionaires-to-be maintained stately homes in Mount Royal while, like so many others, they were living on relief handouts.

Sam Nickle Sr. was the archetypical gambling oil man. Long before anyone recognized the worth of the Athabasca oil sands, he had a lease there. He went broke with it. In Turner Valley he drilled a well to 10,200 feet, the deepest well in the Empire at that time. It's still there. It never yielded anything.

When all seemed lost, Sam somehow got a $5 million bank loan to buy refinery and gasoline outlets. His company, Anglo-American, went into production, refining and sales. Before the multinational giants took over, Anglo-American was the last of the wholly-integrated independent Canadian oil companies.

Eric Harvie was a lawyer for a British company that went broke. As payment for services rendered, he accepted mineral rights in lieu of cash. For years he struggled to hold onto them. When the Leduc and Redwater fields were discovered, he held the mineral rights over great areas of both of them.

Frank and George McMahon were one-rig drilling contractors in Turner Valley. They parlayed that, after Leduc, into Pacific Petroleums. It was another instance of Turner Valley know-how paying off.

The contributions of the successful oil men to the community are vast. They keep a low profile now, often filtering their contributions through charitable or artistic foundations. The Nickle Foundation is one. The Harvie family has pumped millions into the Glenbow Foundation. The McMahons built McMahon Stadium.

Thanks to freer tax laws, a broader base, and an inexhaustible supply of cash, the U.S.-based multinationals control the lion's share of the oil industry today. The oil itself, however, remains more valuable than ever, and the debate is joined about how to make the most out of it. The resolution of this issue directly affects Calgary far more than any other city in the country.

Oil and gas should remain highly valuable commodities well into the foreseeable future. If all else fails, everyone presumably could go back to using crude oil as a laxative.

Surging up — and out

RECORD BUILDING-DEMOLITION UNDERWAY IN CALGARY — NEWS ITEM

NOSE CREEK CONSTRUCTION

NOSE CREEK DEMOLITION CO LTD

"Okay you men . . . put your backs to it . . . they're gaining on us!"
— Tom Innes, 1974

The most obvious change in Calgary since the Leduc oil discovery is simply that there are a lot more Calgarians. An urban population of 129,-000 in 1951 sprouted to 250,000 in 1961 and 398,000 in 1971. A gain of at least 1,000 souls per month became normal, not exceptional. Now, for better or worse, the half-million mark is not only attainable but pretty well inevitable.

Such an input of additional bodies over a long period of time can create a feeling of copelessness — an inability to cope.

Art Evans is an ex-Calgarian who moved north to write a daily column of social comment for The Edmonton Journal. Born in the east end of Calgary in 1919, he grew up there and remembers well what it was like before Leduc. The CPR roundhouse cast a "tattletale grey" over everything. "Some great odors" emanated from the Burns packing plant, the stockyards, the brewery, a soap factory, and the Imperial Oil refinery.

But nobody ever seemed to complain about the soot, the smell and the noise. It was part of everyday life at a time when everything was more personal, and more intimate. Patrons of the Shamrock beer parlor could look out the window and see who was on the train passing by. People still waved at the engineers, and the engineers waved back.

When he comes back to Calgary now, Evans says, it just isn't the same:

"I don't feel as if I'm coming home any more. The population doubles, and triples, and you look around, and you don't know where you are. Paddy

Nolan and Bob Edwards probably wouldn't fit in here now."

Though some neighborhoods here and there haven't changed all that much, and Nolan and Edwards still might find an accommodating corner in a friendly bar somewhere, the Leduc discovery and the discoveries that followed it indeed changed just about everything. They became a cornucopia spilling material benefits all over the landscape, and the landscape inevitably never could be the same again.

The post-Leduc city might have chosen the horn of plenty as a suitable symbol, but instead adopted as its crowning glory the white hat. The defenceless heads of distinguished visitors are decorated with white hats at every opportunity. In return they are required to submit to an "oath of allegiance."

The gesture isn't always appreciated, particularly the third or fourth time around. Prince Philip, for one, felt obliged to say, firmly, that he has enough white hats for now, thank you, and he doesn't want any more.

The combination of black gold and white hats causes the always-busy image makers to equate Calgary, the oil capital, with Dallas, Texas. Like Dallas, Calgary has cows and petroleum, overnight millionaires, cantankerous conservatives, and large, blustery, outspoken characters of all types. It

has always been thus, but latterly everything seems to emerge on a larger stage.

The mayor of Calgary through the 1950s, when the fruit of the oil boom began falling off the derricks, was Don Mackay. Large and loquacious, he began the practice of giving away white hats, and he became himself a white-hatted symbol of the city. He lives in Phoenix, Ariz., now, but gets back to Calgary occasionally. The 1950s "set the cornerstone" for the development of the city, he says today, and he recalls how it all started:

"When the city first began to explode, some local oil people suggested I go to Dallas, which had had a similar experience. I went, and talked to the mayor there, and he predicted 'you will have tall buildings upon tall buildings.' By the time I returned, I'm automatically a visionary gone wild."

Some of the inspiration for the post-Leduc city thus indeed came from Dallas. The new oil capital, it quickly developed, did acquire tall buildings upon tall buildings. It was more than a vision. "I must admit," says Mackay, "it has gone beyond even my wildest dreams."

He got some good advice in Dallas. Annex the surrounding municipalities, the mayor there told him, so the city could retain a single identity. And build out, square mile by square mile, without the kind of leapfrogging that creates awkward and unsightly gaps.

Seducing the neighboring towns took time. Under Mayors Harry Hays (1959-63) and Grant MacEwan (1963-65), Forest Lawn, Montgomery and Bowness finally succumbed. The city limits were pushed out beyond Midnapore to the south, and Calgary avoided the bane of so many other cities that find themselves growing not as a unit but as a lot of separate, squabbling entities.

Among other benefits, annexation eliminated the need for five mayors and five police chiefs. Squabbling continues, but at least it's confined to one city council and one city hall. The impression is that one is enough, or maybe more than enough.

While he was mayor, Harry Hays (later appointed to the Senate after serving as federal minister of agriculture from 1963 to 1965) tried to devise ways to "let people get to work." He tried to move the railway tracks north to the Bow River. That would have cleared the way for a wagon-wheel system of roads leading into, out of, and around the city centre.

Prince Philip gets (another) white hat, this one from Mayor Rod Sykes. Philip thought he had had enough of them.

Town planner Thomas Mawson would have approved. He suggested something similar in 1912. And Napoleon Bonaparte would have approved. He used a wagon wheel to lay out beautiful downtown Paris.

But Calgary always has resisted attempts to transform it into the Paris of the Prairies. The tracks stayed where they were. More and more office and apartment towers jostled for space between the tracks and the river. The traffic flow downtown dropped far below what it should be until, during rush hours, it often hardly seemed to be moving at all.

To get the Glenmore Causeway built in 1961-62, the city council had to employ sleight-of-hand and semantics. To erect a bridge would have required a plebiscite. So they called it a causeway (or roadway) and that didn't require a plebiscite.

The growth of the city is exemplified by Hays Farm. In 1925, the 1,000-acre farm was 4½ miles south of the city limits. Annexed in 1952-53, it became the Haysboro subdivision. The Hays Farm homesite today isn't a farm at all. It's a low-rise apartment development.

Contending with non-stop expansion has preoccupied, and often baffled, every civic administration since 1947. The city acquired parking meters in 1948, one-way streets in 1954, its first parking structure (the Bay Parkade) in 1956, the 8th Ave. mall in 1968, and the convention centre and mall extension in 1974.

Significant post-Leduc additions that have changed the face of the city as a whole include the Jubilee Auditorium, the new General, Rockyview and Foothills hospitals, the Stampede Corral and grandstand, the University of Calgary, McMahon Stadium, a new central library, post office, police station and civic administration building, the Centennial (1967) Planetarium, and the new Mount Royal College in Lincoln Park.

The first industrial parks, Manchester and Highfield, were started in the early 1950s. Downtown, the high-rise laws had to be changed in 1958 to accommodate Elveden House's 20 storeys. Until then the highest building in town was the 12-storey Palliser Hotel.

Now the flagpole height of a few downtown towers challenges even the Calgary Tower. Lacking a better solution, the time could come when the downtown highrises will have to be "frozen" — because there no longer will be any way to get to

Don Mackay was mayor in the '50s.

and from all of them. Traffic could bog down altogether, with motorists just sitting there leaning on their horns in perpetuity.

Narrow streets testify to the fact the town never was planned to accommodate half a million people. The Calgary Transit System has buses called BABES (Blue Arrow Bus Express Service) but pulling teeth is easier than extracting Calgarians from their beloved cars. More than any other city on the continent, this has become a city of cars.

There are approximately 255,000 registered cars and trucks in Calgary. That's more vehicles per capita than anywhere else. Adding to the merriment are about 52,000 registered motorcycles

Land fill stretches more than half way across the reservoir as the
Glenmore Causeway is constructed.

and trailers. With its much larger population, Los Angeles can't match these figures on a per-capita basis.

It has been suggested that what the city needs is a network of bicycle paths and ski trails. And more parks. Downtown, where at last count there were merely 5½ acres of developed parkland, the impression of a concrete jungle is inescapable.

When it isn't being torn up, redesigned, or otherwise out of order, the mall attracts noon-hour crowds of jean-jacketed youths, business-suited executives and mini-skirted secretaries. With everyone competing for a place to sit, walk, or just stand, it represents at best an uneasy sort of togetherness.

While other cities have gone underground, Calgary looks for a respite 15 feet up. Mini-parks at that altitude, with others planned 45 feet up, provide sanctuaries here and there. The Plus-15 concept which links buildings with skywalks has been widely applauded by town planners. It doesn't do anything for the view down in the street. Fully developed, though, it should help ease congestion.

Between downtown and the city limits, Calgary remains mostly a city of homes. The ratio may be changing, but in 1971 single detached dwellings outnumbered apartments two to one. It's perhaps comforting to know that all but 320 of 121,155 dwelling units listed in 1971 offered the convenience of a flush toilet.

An academic study group quite recently undertook to try to define what kind of city post-Leduc Calgary has become. The result was a very informative, fact-packed booklet entitled *Calgary: An Urban Study*.

"Commerce," the researchers concluded, "is what Calgary is all about." That's both good and not so good. The commerce-oriented skyline is a minor jungle of high-rises which "are not particularly pleasing from an aesthetic point of view." However, they are "certainly imposing."

By lumping together various categories, including government, it's possible to demonstrate that almost half of the Calgary labor force is employed in service industries. Comparatively, manufacturing accounts for 13.11 per cent, retail trade for about 10 per cent, construction for about 10 per cent, oil and gas for 9.10 per cent, and wholesale trade for 7.23 per cent.

Harry Hays wanted to move the railway
tracks when he was mayor.

Manufacturing's 13.11 per cent is not a high total, but it is an important part of the over-all picture. Lacking Hamilton-sized steel plants, Sarnia-sized petrochemical plants or Windsor-sized auto plants, Calgary does have a gratifying diversity of small, secondary industries. For aesthetic and other reasons they're preferable to the big, ugly kind.

Reflecting the commerce theme, the city ranks third in Canada in the number of head offices situated here. Toronto has 118, Montreal 84, Calgary 34. Most are in the downtown sector. The academic study found that downtown Calgary, unlike many other modern cities, has managed to remain "dynamic and vital."

The city has its commercial strips (the Macleod Trail, for one) and shopping centres (more than 80 of them, ranging in size from modest to monstrous). It's an extraordinarily far-flung city. But downtown, despite everything, is alive and well.

The new construction speaks for itself. It's sometimes hard to tell who is winning the race, the construction crews or the demolition crews. What's here today may be gone tomorrow. Wherever a vacant lot can be found, it likely won't be a vacant lot the day after tomorrow.

The university researchers concluded that Calgary "would appear to be on the threshold of metropolitan status." Actually, the place is long since over the threshold. A metropolis is defined as "the chief or capital city of a country, state or region." This is the chief city of a large region, and has been for a considerable number of years.

The provincial government would like to slow the growth of the big cities and let the smaller towns grow. Such an arrangement might make everybody happier. But how do you keep them down on the farm, it has to be wondered, when there are amenities only big cities can provide?

Large numbers of people from surrounding towns come regularly to the city to shop, to work, to see a football game or attend a concert. En route, they may pass a lot of city dwellers trying to get away from it all. But the tendency, unless someone finds a practical way to reverse it, is for big cities to just keep getting bigger.

Despite everything, this city still may be close enough to its past to appreciate it. Restoration of the old Fort Calgary site, long overdue, is finally under way. If you can ignore the adjacent junk-

Rush hour traffic over the new Langevin Bridge.

yards and look at the trees instead, it's still possible to visualize the scene as it once was.

In 1974, Calgary acquired the big new convention centre in the east end of downtown. It sounds like a typical venture for a commerce-oriented city, but one element gives it a different dimension. A large part of the new complex will be occupied in 1975 by the Glenbow Alberta Institute.

In its new home Glenbow may, as anticipated, become one of the world's great museums. Meanwhile, the institute has collected and preserved the story of Western Canada from the earliest days. Thanks to Glenbow, future generations will have a chance to know what it was all about.

The Calgary airport handles close to 100 scheduled flights a day.

Quietly, often anonymously, and often without any thanks, the millionaires of Calgary have pumped millions of dollars back into their community. The Glenbow Foundation was started by Eric Harvie in 1955. He collected art, books, and artifacts literally by the truck load — everything he could get his hands on — and wound up with the most complete record of the history of Western Canada in existence anywhere.

In 1966, the Harvie family turned the collection over to the Alberta government. The Glenbow Alberta Institute, charged with establishing and administering museums and art galleries, and with carrying on the search for artifacts, was launched with matching $5 million grants from the family and the province.

All the institute has lacked, until now, has been a home to call its own. Part of it formerly occupied the old Hull Estate. That was torn down and the Hull Estate today is an immense apartment building. The Glenbow collection was strewn all over the city — the library and archives in the old sandstone library in Central park, a museum in the old sandstone court house on 7th Ave., an art gallery on 11th Ave., and warehouses scattered hither and yon.

The institute owns 25,000 books and 100,000 photographs. It owns paintings, drawings, sculptures, prints, film, tape, and antiques of every description. Much of the collection is stored away in crates, on display racks, and in workshops. New acquisitions, still by the truck load, keep pouring in faster than a dedicated staff can cope with them.

The space allocated to Glenbow in the convention centre means the institute finally will be able to bring together its art gallery, museum, library, archives, and everything else. Within 10 years it's confidently predicted, the Glenbow collection will bear comparison with anything similar anywhere in the world, including such historic capitals as London and Paris.

Perhaps, to a degree, Calgary deserves the image of a city with a big dollar sign hanging over it, but it's impossible to put a dollar value on something like Glenbow.

Calgary's soaring skyline: what a difference a century makes!

Epilogue

No one knows, of course, where the city goes from here. After 100 years, a clear image of what to expect isn't readily discernible. But more people are caring now about shaping the scene in a desirable way.

It becomes a matter of enhancing that elusive thing called the quality of life. If Calgary is a good place to live, and most Calgarians think it is, the trick is to keep it good and, wherever possible, make it better. In this sense it's not really moving away from the material but it's putting much more emphasis on the human qualities of life.

In 1875, all of Calgary-to-be was one vast natural park. As described by the Mounties, the site of the present city was covered with long grass and numerous small lakes swarming with wild fowl. The river banks were all flanked by trees, and wild game of all kinds was plentiful.

In 1974, the city was frantically trying to rescue and preserve at least some of that original park. That people care was demonstrated when the government circulated a questionnaire asking what should be done with the new Fish Creek park. There were an astonishing 30,000 replies.

In 1875, 50 Mounties huddled in trenches near the junction of the Bow and Elbow Rivers. Their first thought was to build — specifically to build a fort and get warm before winter set in.

The idea of growth for its own sake took over in the present century. The population in 1900 still was only about 4,000. The real-estate and building boom that peaked in 1912 encouraged the notion that this was going to be another Chicago. In 1974, that kind of dream seemed more like a nightmare.

Now, before it's too late, the city looks back and treasures its past. Heritage Park provides authentic reminders of how it was in the not-so-distant past. The frontier spirit is cherished. Because the place is so young, the frontier still isn't really so far away.

But, being practical about it, can any city really turn its back on growth? The best guess probably is no. Only a viable, growing economy can support such luxuries as museums and the arts. Or a professional football team. Now both the past and the future demand to be taken into account in finding a happy, livable medium between cowtown and metropolis.

From the start Calgary has attracted a rich and colorful diversity of individuals. Any city would be hard pressed to match a cast of characters that includes Macleod, Crowfoot, Lacombe, Col. Walker, the Big Four, Bob Edwards, Paddy Nolan, Cappy Smart, R. B. Bennett, and William Aberhart.

The enterprise of these individuals isn't necessarily lacking in the modern era. The way in which the McMahons and Red Dutton built themselves a ball park is characteristic. The way in which a mob of Calgarians went east to get the 1975 Grey Cup game (Ottawa, dismayed by the westerners' zeal, withdrew its bid) reflected some of the 1948 spirit.

If others think of this place as Dallas North, full of hidebound millionaires, it's unfortunate. In this respect, the Stampede may be the city's salvation. If there has to be an image, there are worse images, however far-fetched it may be today, than that of the free-wheeling, fun-loving cowboy.

Calgary lacks Vancouver's ocean, Toronto's size, scope and influence, a ballet company like Winnipeg's, and Montreal's cosmopolitanism. But, here and there, progress is being made. Surprisingly, perhaps, there are 30 commercial art galleries in Calgary. That's 30 more than 100 years ago.

The last frontier, or what's left of it, never has appreciated outside help in contending with its problems and shortcomings, real or imagined. In recent years, looking at the rather indiscriminate growth all around them, Calgarians themselves have become healthily concerned.

In the old days, people would complain that they didn't know everybody in town any more, the place was just getting so darned big. Now it isn't just the people. Now it's possible to walk past monumental office buildings and find you can't even put a name to them, let alone know who works there.

As a city, maybe this one remains something of a diamond in the rough — brash, a bit loud, and occasionally a bit crude. But there always have been such mitigating factors as the mountains and the Chinook. Such man-made additions as the Jubilee Auditorium, the University of Calgary, Mount Royal College, the Planetarium, the Calgary Philharmonic and Theatre Calgary all help to smooth the rough edges.

Wander around, and you still can discover some of the flavor of the old town. It's in the east end of downtown, in a few of the older residential districts, and down by the stockyards. The cowboy tradition, aside from the Stampede, is out in the country, in High River, Claresholm, Longview, and in the foothills to the west.

The year of the Centennial, 1975, provides an opportunity to look back and contemplate what has happened here. It has been a lively, onward-and-upward 100 years. If the youngster sired by the Mounties has been a bit of a brat sometimes, that child left a worthwhile legacy.

If it's now time to mature and ripen into middle age, so be it.

Painting illustrates what Calgary probably looked like in 1867; below,
the same view of Calgary, 1967.

Acknowledgments

Many individuals have helped make this book possible through what they have written over previous years, their own recollections in interviews, and the research material they have made available. To thank all of them individually is impractical. There are too many of them.

Particular thanks are extended to Hugh A. Dempsey, director of history at Glenbow, and Calgary author James H. Gray, who read the first draft and suggested improvements. They contributed a great deal toward making it a good deal better and more complete than it otherwise might have been.

Much of the raw research material came from the Glenbow-Alberta Foundation and the files of The Calgary Herald, fleshed out by interviews with a large number of individuals who gave freely of their time and particular knowledge about Calgary and its history. The courtesy and helpfulness of the staff of the Glenbow Foundation is particularly appreciated.

The assistance of Herald editor-in-chief, Richard Sanburn, in preparing the text, and that of Lorne Kennedy, promotion and public relations manager, in the actual production of the book was invaluable, as was the help of a great many people in The Herald newsroom who volunteered their services.

For those who might like to pursue the subject in greater detail, the following books are recommended for further reading:

The North-West Mounted Police 1873-1893, John Peter Turner, Queen's Printer, Ottawa, 1950.

Maintain The Right, Ronald Atkin, Macmillan, 1973.

Calgary Cavalcade, Grant MacEwan, The Institute of Applied Art Ltd., Edmonton, 1958.

Calgary, W. B. Fraser, Holt, Rinehart and Winston of Canada Ltd., 1967.

Crowfoot, Hugh A. Dempsey, Hurtig Publishers, 1972.

The National Dream, Pierre Berton, McClelland and Stewart.

Tales of The Old Town, Leishman McNeill, Calgary Herald.

The Range Men, Leroy V. Kelly, Calgary Herald.

50 Mighty Men, Grant MacEwan, Modern Press, Saskatoon, 1958.

Our Alberta Heritage, Jacques Hamilton, Calgary Power, 1971.

Calgary in Sandstone, Richard Cunniffe, Historical Society of Alberta, 1969.

Eye-Opener Bob, Grant MacEwan, Institute of Applied Art, 1957.

The Winter Years, James H. Gray, Macmillan, 1966.

Red Lights on The Prairies, James H. Gray, Macmillan, 1971.

Booze, James H. Gray, Macmillan, 1972.

10 Lost Years, Barry Broadfoot, Doubleday, 1973.

The Wretched of Canada, Michael Bliss, University of Toronto, 1971.

The Social Credit Movement in Alberta, John A. Irving, University of Toronto Press, 1959.

Social Credit and The Party System, C. B. MacPherson, University of Toronto Press, 1953.

Singing Wires, Tony Cashman, Alberta Government Telephones, 1972.

The Calgary Stampede Story, Fred Kennedy, T. E. Thonger, 1952.

The Story of Pincher Creek and Turner Valley, Carl O. Nickle, The Daily Oil Bulletin, Calgary.

Calgary: An Urban Study, Richard P. Baine, Clarke, Irwin & Co., 1973.

Index:

This is Bob Shiels' first book after many years as a newspaper writer. Bob has been at home in the newsroom since 1948 when he joined the editorial staff of his home-town Medicine Hat News, "covering everything due to being the only reporter on the staff."

In 1950 he moved to Edmonton and for three years covered the Legislature for The Journal. Next came The Windsor Star where he spent the better part of two years covering that city's civic affairs.

On a spring day in 1955, Bob Shiels arrived in The Calgary Herald newsroom, and between then and the writing of this book, he has covered everything from the oil beat to the making of a Doris Day movie in Hollywood. In recent years Herald readers have followed his daily television columns.

Picture Credits

The majority of photographs appearing in this book were obtained either from the Glenbow-Alberta Institute or from The Calgary Herald picture files. The editors also wish to acknowledge pictures from the Ernest Brown collection and the Harry Pollard collection, printed with the permission of the Alberta provincial archives in Edmonton. Two photographs in the "Get-up-and-go times" chapter were obtained from the Calgary Transit System. A photograph of Fred McCall in the cockpit of his plane (page 144) was contributed by Kenneth Hyde of Hyde Aerial-Industrial Photography. A great many of the pictures were taken by Herald staff photographers, past and present, and in many respects, this book is a tribute to their initiative through the years.